FACETS OF THE
ENGLISH SCENE

Other titles by Garry Hogg:

Castles of England

Customs and Traditions of England

A Guide to English Country Houses

Odd Aspects of England

Priories and Abbeys of England

Inns and Villages of England

London in Colour

The Shell Book of Exploring Britain

Facets of the
English Scene

GARRY HOGG

DAVID & CHARLES : NEWTON ABBOT

0 7153 5880 4

Set in 12pt Plantin by
W J Holman Limited Dawlish
and printed in Great Britain
by Biddles Limited Guildford
for David & Charles (Holdings) Limited
South Devon House Newton Abbot Devon

Contents

	Author's Foreword	.	.	.	.	.	6
1.	Toll Houses	.	.	.	.	.	8
2.	Lych-Gates	.	.	.	.	.	14
3.	Topiary Work	.	.	.	.	.	22
4.	Wrought-iron Inn Signs	.	.	.	.	26
5.	Walls and Stiles	.	.	.	.	.	32
6.	Thatch	.	.	.	.	.	38
7.	Tombstones	.	.	.	.	.	44
8.	Churchyard Crosses	.	.	.	.	52
9.	Signposts and Milestones	.	.	.	.	56
10.	Rock Monsters	.	.	.	.	.	64
11.	Buildings	.	.	.	.	.	70
12.	Miscellany	.	.	.	.	.	86
	Map	.	.	.	.	.	108
	Index	.	.	.	.	.	110

Author's Foreword

A country is ordinarily depicted in terms of its major features. In the case of England one would range in a broad sweep over its strongly contrasted regions: the harsh granite uplands of Dartmoor and Bodmin Moor in the West Country; the gentler chalk country of Sussex; the mountains, fells and valleys of the Lake District; the open spaces along the Pennine Chain from Derbyshire to the Tyne; the hunting shires of the Midlands; the mellow countryside adjoining the Welsh Marches; the hop-gardens and cherry orchards of Kent; East Anglia, with its little known Breckland and better known Broads; the Dales of Yorkshire's North Riding; the forests of Kielder and the Cheviot slopes; the limestone country of the Cotswolds. And so forth.

This, of course, has all been done before, a hundred times over; I have done it myself in **The Shell Book of Exploring Britain,** in which I did in fact step across the border northwards into Scotland and westwards into Wales. But in that book the approach was different, more sweeping, less concerned with what could be called the **minutiae,** the intimate detail. In the present book, however, I have returned to the detailed portrayal, the approach (though the details do not overlap) which was the mainspring of my **Odd Aspects of England.** After all, the total impact of any country on those who, whether native or from overseas, set out to explore it is twofold: there is the broad immediate impression; and there is also the cumulative effect of the details of particularity, of which the sightseer is perhaps at first hardly even aware. It may be the sum total of these that conditions his response to the whole.

For every individual who carries away the strongest impression of, say, the lush pastureland of Herefordshire or, by contrast, the gritstone 'Edges' of Derbyshire, there will be another on whom the more intimate detail of a medieval lych-gate, an ancient churchyard cross with a 'story' to tell, or a length of apparently commonplace walling that speaks of an old tradition of craftsmanship cherished right through into this highly mechanised and commercialised age, makes the deepest impression. Or so, at least, I myself believe—or I would never have compiled this particular record of what there is to be seen.

Inevitably (and I make no apology here) the contents of this book reflect one individual's tastes. In assembling material for it I pursued my own fancies, believing (I hope rightly) that there must be many, particularly among the camera-minded, who are endowed with something of the collector's pleasure in looking for, locating, and eventually pinning down, like butterflies on an entomologist's cork panels, those odd items of the English rural scene which happen to have aroused curiosity and speculation. One man's meat is of course another man's —well, if not poison, at least less-well-regarded dish. But the sheer variety of collectors' pieces in one form or another, scattered widely about the country, is so great that anyone can easily satisfy himself with **trouvailles** that another might reject. In this book alone I have, for one reason or another, discarded more material than I have included.

Speaking of **trouvailles**—things 'found'—not all can be said to fall into any immediately obvious category. I have therefore taken the easy way out and headed the last section, quite simply, 'Miscellany'. This is a sort of negative category; a mish-mash (to use an old-fashioned pleasant term) of items that are not easy to accommodate in specific categories but which may, individually, spark off interest and prompt further individual research.

The process is simple, and pleasurable. A few hundred miles of judicious driving, with a large-scale map beside you as well as your camera, perhaps a congenial passenger to spot details that, while concentrating on your driving, you might just miss, and you will be well on the way to expanding and elaborating any one of the dozen categories in this book, and, doubtless, adding some new ones of your own. I myself rarely venture forth, whether in my own country or abroad, without an arsenal of cameras and a sheaf of large-scale maps. I have compiled this book primarily for readers who also take pleasure in keeping their own record of places visited and simple things enjoyed. Within a hundred odd pages it cannot do more than touch the fringe of its theme; indeed, my hope is that it will not so much satisfy curiosity as stimulate interest in what is virtually an inexhaustible field.

G.H.

Groombridge, Sussex

Acknowledgements

My thanks are due to the Chief Librarian of the British Tourist Authority for permission to include the two photographs at the top of page 73 and the ones at the top right and bottom of page 101. Also to Messrs Whitbread & Co, Ltd, for permission to include the photograph at the bottom of page 73, and to the Corporation of Hastings for permission to include the photograph on page 85. I took the remaining 129 photographs specially for this book.

7

I. TOLL HOUSES

Throughout the eighteenth and early nineteenth centuries Turnpike Trusts proliferated: set up, usually by 'interested parties', and backed by special Acts of Parliament, their function was to maintain in good repair sections of through-roads linking market town with market town, one focal point of communal life with another. These were the Turnpike Roads, whose total mileage eventually exceeded 20,000. But the maintenance of roads cost money, and the Turnpike Acts empowered the Trustees to exact dues from drovers and wagoners, stage-coach and private carriage owners, and pedestrians; these dues (which caused much anger and hostility) were exacted at the toll houses established at the beginning of each stretch of turnpike road. The turnpike-men exacted the toll; and the tolls, in gross, enabled the Trustees eventually to develop a road system that was an echo of the great days of the Roman occupation centuries earlier, and was to form the basis of our own vast network in the present busy century.

Very many toll houses still survive, though only a handful still fulfil their original function. Unhappily, road-widening projects threaten many of them with extinction, but those still standing are easy to identify. Set close to the road, a porch or window almost on the road itself, and often at a road junction or where the carriageway is fairly narrow, they are usually hexagonal, octagonal or round, compact, well windowed both up and down the road, and bear a curious air of alertness, even though the last turnpikemen worked there generations ago.

Devizes, Wiltshire. A Victorian specimen, this, at the fork of the A 361 and A 342 roads on the western outskirts of the town. With heavy castellation, ornate window-moulding and of fortress-like solidity, it is not surprising that it is locally known (though no one can explain the actual name) as 'Shane's Castle'. It ceased to be a toll house in 1889, when one George Brown lived there. His name, and the address, appear in the Devizes **Directory** for that year. It has been privately occupied ever since, and is so to this day. You might think that, with traffic to Bath and Chippenham on either side, it would be too noisy to live in; but its walls are immensely thick and its windows small. The present occupier states that he is well content to live out his last years in Shane's Castle.

(Top left) **Nr Warden, Northumberland,** 2 miles north-west of Hexham. This most attractive stone-built and slate-roofed toll house stands on a corner, against the west rampart of the bridge spanning the South Tyne. It is—as the photograph clearly shows—occupied by someone who has gone out of his (or her) way to make the little single-storey house more than just habitable. The white-painted door has iron studs in it and a pair of ornate wrought-iron hinges and handles to match. Hexagonal in the main, it has a stone gabled portion abutting on to it and on to the bridge.

(Top right) **Nr Bishop's Cleeve, Gloucestershire,** 3 miles north of Cheltenham, on A 435. The half-hexagonal front has been extended rearwards to increase accommodation for the present occupants. They take pleasure in retaining the faded signboard in the 'blind' window, which reads: 'For every horse or mule not drawing, 2d; on a Sunday, 3d. For every horse, mule or other beast of draught drawing any coach, chaise, phaeton, curricle, gig or waggon, 6d; and on a Sunday, 9d'. Clearly travel, whether for business or for pleasure, on the Lord's Day was frowned upon in this locality.

(Bottom left) **Nr Honiton, Devon.** There seems some doubt as to why this toll house, on the Axminster road, A 373, a mile west of Honiton, should be named 'Copper Castle': certainly there is no evidence of copper. With its castellations nicely picked out in black on white, its rounded 'bows' fronting a busy road, and an oddly shaped 'porthole' offset above the narrow door, it catches the eye unexpectedly. Perhaps, technically, its major feature is a pair of nineteenth-century wrought-iron gates (now never used) in place of the traditional five-barred wooden gate.

(Bottom right) **Tavistock, Devon.** This extremely well preserved specimen of a completely slate-hung toll house stands on the Launceston road, A 384, on the outskirts of the town. Eight-sided and two-storeyed, it is externally faced with slate 'from top to toe'. It is probably safe to generalise and say that the majority of the toll houses that have now passed into private occupation have been painted white and brightened all over; this one presents a more sombre appearance, but for all that it has an attractiveness all its own.

10

(Top left) **Nr Stanton Drew, Somerset,** 6 miles south of Bristol, on B 3130. Almost opposite a garage, marking the turning off to the prehistoric Stone Circles of Stanton Drew and Hautville's Quoit, it stands on a small triangle of turf, its five sides cream-stuccoed beneath a circular thatched roof. Set against the small doorway facing the larger of the two roads is a diminutive pillar-box, its opening sufficient only, one would say, for letters written to and by dwarfs. Over the porch is the bracket from which formerly hung a lamp to enable the toll-house keeper to inspect the payment offered by wayfarers.

(Top right) **Nr Chard, Somerset.** This toll house stands in a tight angle between the A 30 road to the west and a minor road branching south-westwards, to the west of the town. Its fabric is, most unusually, of pebbles inset in stone forming ten large panels, each containing a Gothic-arched door or window. A ten-sided thatched roof with very wide overhanging eaves is supported by ten stout larch poles inset in the cobbled surround. So deep are the eaves that one can walk right round the building beneath their shelter. The door, facing the junction of the roads, is nail-studded.

(Bottom) **Swinford Toll Bridge, nr Eynsham, Oxfordshire.** It carries the A 4141 road from Oxford to the main A 40, short of Witney. It complacently announces that it has been 'designated as of special architectural and historical interest'. It dates from 1765 and therefore its original signboard was much older than the present one, which refers to George III and the 'Locomotive Act of 1861'. Mechanically propelled vehicles, it states, are charged at the rate of 5d for every ton gross or fraction thereof; all other vehicles are charged at the rate of 1d per wheel. Pedestrians are not charged. Cyclists, until recently, paid the penny-per-wheel due; now they go free also. And there is another concession; at midnight the gate is opened fully, and all traffic passes over Swinford Bridge without let or hindrance. This toll house is privately owned and, as elsewhere, the owner is reluctant in the extreme to state what the takings are worth to him as an annual source of income. Nor, in the circumstances, is this entirely to be wondered at.

2. LYCH-GATES

Though they ordinarily have a venerable air, and indeed often suggest antiquity and not mere age, lych-gates are almost all of relatively recent date. They may give access to medieval, Norman or even Saxon churches, but they themselves will probably date from the seventeenth or eighteenth century. They are almost as numerous as the thousands of churches dotted about England, for there are few country churches, at any rate, that are not approached by way of these pleasing and diversified structures.

Their evolution is interesting. **Lych** is Anglo-Saxon for corpse: thus a lych-gate is literally a corpse-gate. The corpse (in medieval times not coffined but shrouded) was laid by its bearers in the church precincts to await the bier and priest. So, a stone of adequate dimensions for the corpse to be laid on it was positioned against the stile which was the normal entrance to the churchyard since it could be negotiated by human beings but not by sheep and cattle. A good surviving example of such a stone may be seen at Luxulyan, Cornwall: an enormous locally quarried granite boulder, roughly hewn, on which, down the centuries a succession of corpses awaited the bier. There is no lych-gate, but the corpse-stone is only a few yards from the church.

In due course the awkward stile was generally replaced by a gate, and, since bearers and mourners did not relish waiting about in bad weather on these mournful occasions, a roof of some sort was erected for their comfort. A true craftsman takes pride in exercising his skills to the best of his ability; he would undoubtedly have been encouraged in this by the lord of the manor, the squire, the priest-in-charge, or other local interested party, for the design and construction and ornamentation of the lych-gate was a matter of local pride and even of county competition. You will never find two lych-gates exactly alike; and this is as it should be. You may find some over ornate for your taste, some may give the impression of being over large for the church to which they give access, and sometimes the materials used do not marry too well with those mainly used in the buildings close to the church—heavy tiles, perhaps, where most roofs are thatched, or cold slate where russet handmade tiles predominate—but it will be hard to find a lych-gate, however unassuming, that does not possess some memorable feature. It may be its sheer simplicity of design and execution; the delicacy, strength, whimsicality or flowing beauty of its carving; or the ingenuity shown in the operation of a swivel-gate that has

been installed in place of the customary hinged gate, as is often the case in sheep-farming country. There is a neat example of this in Friston, Sussex.

Lych-gates sometimes incorporated dwelling-space, occupied by verger, sexton or even priest. At Bray, Berkshire, a massive brick-and-timber structure over the gate was occupied for a time by the notorious 'Vicar of Bray', Papist-turned-Protestant. At Long Compton, Warwickshire, the lych-gate supports a thatched half-timbered room called the Priest's House and occupied first by a succession of vergers and sextons and, until quite recently, by the village cobbler, of all incongruous tenants.

(Previous page) **St Peter's Church, Ightham, Kent,** 6 miles north of Tonbridge, on A 227. By no means the least attractive feature of this most beautiful Kentish village is its tree-embowered lych-gate. The massive stone block just outside it, on the left, is not the coffin (or corpse) stone; it is in fact a four-step mounting-block, a reminder that in the seventeenth and eighteenth centuries (and even later) members of the congregation, and even the parson himself, might ride to church and have their horses returned to them after the service by their grooms or other servants. There is another such mounting-block at the lych-gate to the ancient Church of St John the Baptist at Stokesay, in Shropshire.

(Opposite) **Holy Trinity Church, Clifton, Derbyshire,** 1 mile south of Ashbourne, on A 515. There may be other lych-gates in the country that have a clock mounted in the apex of their gable, but this is the only one that comes to mind. The church is very much older than its lych-gate, and the lych-gate is considerably older than the clock, which was presented to the church as recently as 1924. Perhaps it was installed in the lych-gate rather than in the tower because the church itself is screened by trees, whereas its lych-gate stands beside the road, so that every passer-by can read the time without the necessity of consulting his watch.

(Top left) **Parish Church, St Just in Roseland, Cornwall,** 8 miles south of Truro, off A 3078. There is no gate beneath the slate roof of this stone-and-timber-built lych-gate, and no coffin-stone, but two slate benches enable you to sit and gaze downwards through the rhododendrons and close-set shrubs at this 700-year-old church or, alternatively, to consider the advice inscribed on one wall:

> Stranger, in peace pursue thine onward road,
> But ne'er forget thy last and long abode . . .

(Top right) **St Michael's, Ilsington, Devon,** 8 miles north-west of Newton Abbot, off A 38. This most attractive lych-gate-cum-gatehouse stands at the top of a village built along a steeply rising street. Though the church is dedicated to St Michael, the figure in the niche on the right is that of St George, a gift commemorating World War I. A granite stairway gives access to the room, which is self-contained and looks both out over the street and inwards over the churchyard. It has its own fireplace and chimney—a very rare feature indeed.

(Bottom left) **Parish Church, Stoke Poges, Buckinghamshire,** 5 miles south of Beaconsfield, on A 473. This is the inner of the two lych-gates giving access to the churchyard which was the setting for Gray's **Elegy.** It is unusual to find two lych-gates to one church, but the tally of gravestones is so great that there is an outer as well as an inner churchyard, the second lych-gate separating the two. Of the two the second is the more pleasing, with its bold yet fluent carving on steeply pitched barge-boards.

(Bottom right) **Church of the Most Holy Trinity, Barsham, Suffolk,** 3 miles west of Beccles, on A 1116. This lych-gate perfectly matches the rural simplicity of the setting, and the church itself. Like the church, it is thatched. Behind it, a short avenue of close-set yew trees marks the narrow path to the south porch. The timber framing above the lintel has been in-filled with plasterwork, and the centre post carries a charming effigy in carved oak of some unnamed saint who smiles soberly downwards on the churchgoers.

3. TOPIARY WORK

Topiary, the art of sculpture in tree or shrub, has flourished in England for more than four centuries. Box and yew have always been the favourites with topiarists, since they are compact, grow evenly, and lend themselves better to the art than such other shrubs as laurel, holly and privet.

The finest examples of the topiarist's art will of course be found in the ornamental gardens of the great houses, the stately homes, of this country. Compton Wynyates, in Warwickshire, is said by some to offer the finest display of topiary in all England; but the 'Sermon on the Mount' at Packwood, also in Warwickshire, the superbly organised yew-tree gardens at Levens Hall, in Westmorland, the display at Montacute, in Somerset, that in the gardens of Long Melford Hall, Suffolk, and several others, all run Compton Wynyates pretty close. To maintain such an array of clipped yew and box, slow in growth as they are, must require the concentrated attention of a whole army of gardener-craftsmen.

Quite apart from the famous and historic examples of topiary in our great houses, however, there are, often in the least expected corners of the country, examples of the work of what might be called non-professional topiarists, many of whom show skill and imagination of no mean order, though their work is on a less grandiose scale. Humble cottagers owning a yew hedge often reveal surprising know-how, and the pleasure they must derive from looking at their handiwork is shared by all who pass by.

(Top) **The Lea, Shropshire,** 5 miles south-east of Clun, off B 4367. This is 'modern' topiary—a locomotive forming part of the boundary hedge of a private house. Somewhat crude, as yet, it will improve with age and careful pruning over the years to come.

(Bottom) **Beckington, Somerset,** 3 miles north of Frome, on A 361. Manifestly this topiary cruiser has been on the stocks for a longer period than the engine. Its lines are more assured, its stern-chaser guns accurately tilted, its radar and other navigating equipment nicely realised and installed. Some idea of its proportions may be gained by comparison with the mini-van beneath its shapely bows.

(Top left) **Sapperton, Gloucestershire,** 6 miles east of Stroud, off A 419. So far as cottage gardens go, birds are the most popular choice of the topiarist, especially the peacock, with its fine crest and spreading tail-feathers. This one is spectacularly perched on a twenty-tier yew column which perhaps displays more skill in the pruning than does the bird itself. Just behind is what appears to be a stork on its nest, also on a twenty-tier column. This, of course, is an appropriate position, since the stork traditionally seeks the highest perch available in the building of its choice—a gabled roof (as at Rothenburg, for instance) or, most popular, a chimney.

(Top right) **Cross, Somerset,** 1 mile west of Axbridge, off A 38. Toad-stools (or what, as Shakespeare wrote, 'our liberal shepherds give a grosser name') rise to the height of the eaves of this cottage lying back from the road; or they might be a group of guardsmen standing sentinel, their bearskins balanced on slender necks and tending to sway slightly when the wind blows up the lane.

(Bottom left) **Micheldean, Gloucestershire,** 4 miles south-east of Ross, on B 4224. The cottager here has perhaps been influenced both by the topiary at Cross and Sapperton, for he seems to have combined the two. His peacock is very much more sophisticated than the Sapperton bird—indeed, it might well be called stylised—but the tiered plinths are less ambitious than those at Cross. The creator, however, has shown originality in that the graduated tiers are square, like slabs of toast or paving-stones, rather than circular, which is more customary.

(Bottom right) **Kempsey, Worcestershire,** 4 miles south of Worcester, on A 38. It is not easy to make up one's mind as to whether this is a bird in sore need of painstaking trimming, or some creature of the topiarist's fancy. Could it be an armadillo? Is it a giant hedgehog with an elongated neck? A tortoise with an improbable head? Or an attempt at an ostrich or emu, its legs not yet developed, or maybe hidden in the clumps beneath the body? No matter. This is a characteristic specimen of the cottage-topiarist's art, and suggests that the sculptor has not yet made up his mind what to evolve from the ubiquitous yew.

4· WROUGHT-IRON INN SIGNS

One might 'collect' inn signs as other people collect stamps or coins. Probably no one could state exactly just how many inns there are in England—certainly their tally runs well into four figures, possibly into five. Because ever since the end of the fourteenth century it has been laid down by law that every innkeeper must display a sign to identify his premises, their variety is almost infinite.

The vast majority are painted boards slung from brackets. They may portray kings' or queens' heads, heraldic emblems, birds, animals (lions are almost always red, bears black rather than brown), or saints and (in the case of certain traditional and therefore well loved figures such as highwaymen) sinners. They may indicate travel: by stagecoach or pack-horse or new-fangled railway, with a forward glance at air travel and—who knows?—the amphibious hovercraft.

Simply to list England's inn signs would be to fill this book twice over. So, for the present purpose, the accent is on a small but distinguished minority of signs—the wrought-iron, or, its close relative, the sheet-iron silhouette. Even with this category the problem, once again, is not what to include but what, reluctantly, to reject.

(Top left) **Snape, Suffolk,** 3 miles south of Saxmundham. The most popular of all heraldic signs, the Crown, frequently bracketed with Rose or Mitre.

(Top right) **Southwold, Suffolk.** A beautiful example of a local blacksmith's craft.

(Middle left) **Altrincham, Cheshire.** Not, strictly, wrought-iron, but stamped out of sheet iron and gilded and then placed in a wrought-iron circle.

(Middle right) **Great Budworth, Cheshire,** 5 miles west of Knutsford. More ornate than that at Altrincham, with an outstandingly beautiful wrought-iron bracket.

(Bottom left) **Farnham, Suffolk,** 2 miles south of Saxmundham. Mounted on a post set well in advance of the inn, to encourage the thirsty traveller looking for refreshment.

(Bottom right) **Cheadle, Cheshire.** You could well miss this altogether, for it hangs out over a traffic-crowded main street. It is worth more than a backward glance.

(Top left) **Snape Bridge, Suffolk,** 4 miles south of Saxmundham. The village, noted for its long tradition of malting, is just inland from the Suffolk coast at Aldeburgh, and the artist-craftsman who designed this attractive sign has contrived to introduce both these aspects within one nicely integrated concept.

(Top right) **Bolney, Sussex,** 8 miles west of Haywards Heath, off A 272. There are innumerable examples of bells—usually in 'peals' of six or eight—up and down the country. These are in fact miniature brass bells, of handbell-ringers' proportions, cleverly hung inside the neat wrought-iron scrollwork.

(Middle left) **St Neots, Huntingdonshire.** The Key was the emblem of St Peter, gatekeeper of Heaven. Here is the 'Cross Keys', but elsewhere the sign may be titled 'Crossed Keys'. There are many of these scattered about the country, but few have the character of this example, or are carried by a bracket of such distinction.

(Middle right) **Chipping Sodbury, Gloucestershire.** An unusual sign, beautifully conceived. The portcullis is accurately riveted, its points sharpened, and the chains by which its prototype, in the main gatehouse of the traditional Norman castle, would have been operated, are skilfully wrought to scale. The whole is enclosed within an iron ring and supported by a very simple but most effective wrought-iron bracket.

(Bottom left) **Lanreath, Cornwall,** 7 miles south-west of Liskeard, off B 3359. This unusually shaped sign invites the traveller to step inside an inn which claims to be four hundred years old and enjoy a bowl of punch—for which, like Cornish mead, it has had a reputation for centuries. It is claimed that the sign now replacing the original one is the work of the late Augustus John, RA.

(Bottom right) **Mere, Wiltshire.** No excuse is offered for including this specimen, though the actual sign is an iron plate inscribed in gold. The justification lies in the quality of the immense wrought-iron bracket that supports it; you may travel the length and breadth of England and not find one that surpasses, or even matches, it in intricacy of design or subtlety of craftsmanship.

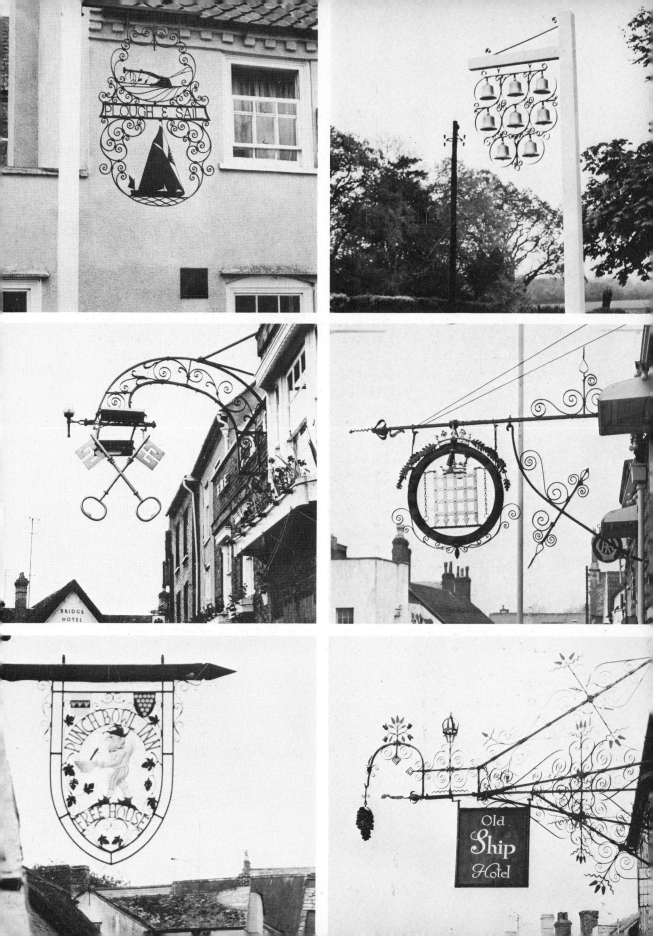

(Top left) **Stonham Parva, Suffolk,** 5 miles east of Stowmarket, on A 140. What are known as 'gallows' signs—those mounted on beams spanning the road beneath—are now rare, removed by Authority as a potential danger to traffic. This is an exception, surprising because the road below carries much fast traffic. Perhaps this fact accounts for the jaunty angle at which the magpie carries its upswept tail.

(Top right) **Harleston, Suffolk.** In this part of England the magpie seems to have come into its own, though it is by no means as widespread generally as the Cock and the Eagle which, with the Swan, must be the three commonest birds on inn signs. This specimen dominates a corner of the marketplace of a busy little town.

(Middle left) **Market Harborough, Leicestershire.** The Swan is almost certainly the most popular of all bird inn signs. Here, at a famous hostelry once run by John Fothergill, two of the swans stand in silhouette, the third on a plaque between them; but perhaps the best feature of the sign is the intricate wrought-ironwork enclosing the central panel.

(Middle right) **Southwold, Suffolk.** Another Swan, not of wrought iron but moulded and three-dimensional, and mounted on an outstandingly beautiful specimen of graduated scrollwork—the handiwork, incidentally, of the blacksmith responsible for that other notable inn sign in Southwold, The Crown.

(Bottom left) **Uppingham, Rutland.** After the Lion, in all probability the Hart—invariably white—is the most frequently seen of all animal signs. This example is modern, the work of an art master at Uppingham School. So delicate is the wrought-ironwork that it might almost be called filigree.

(Bottom right) **Moreton-in-Marsh, Gloucestershire.** A forthright, no-compromise specimen of inn sign-making, with a nice balance between the whiteness of the climbing beast and the blackness of the rock on which its hooves are placed and the antlers that merge into the rectangular wrought-iron panel containing it.

5. WALLS and STILES

A region builds in the materials lying most readily to hand—half-timbering in Cheshire and down the Welsh Border, where oak once grew in abundance; millstone-grit and carboniferous limestone in Lancashire and the West and North Ridings of Yorkshire; slate in Cumberland, Westmorland and Cornwall; granite in Cornwall and west Devonshire; oolitic limestone in the Cotswolds and along the belt spanning England from Axminster to Flamborough Head; flint in East Anglia and parts of Sussex and Surrey. The 'feel' of a region can be sensed as soon as its outlier walls are recognised. This is particularly the case in the Pennines, where the intricate network of drystone walling meets the eye often from a hill-brow or across a valley.

Cornwall boasts slate and granite, each of which, over the centuries, has dictated the method of its utilisation. Slate, though a sedimentary rock, is rarely laid (as far as walls are concerned) horizontally. It is laid on edge, 'shoulder to shoulder', like closely-packed books on a shelf, and turfed over. As a picturesque alternative it is laid in zigzag courses, to produce a 'herringbone' effect, like a strongly emphasised tweed seen under a magnifying glass. This, too, is turf-topped, flower-grown. Less picturesque, but most imposing, is the granite wall. Irregularly shaped blocks weighing up to 2 cwt and more are piled, seemingly without plan, though in fact with skill and precision as well as strength, to produce walls that can vie with the so-called 'Cyclopean' walls at the fortress of Tiryns, on the road to Mycenae, and at Mycenae itself. Such wall-building, whether in England or in Greece, tacitly implies a race of giant builders.

(Top and Middle) **Nr Stratton, Cornwall,** 2 miles east of Bude, off A 39. A length of 'herringbone' slate wall bounding private property from public highway. A dozen courses, each pitched at 45 degrees to the vertical, are so well matched (as can be seen in the close-up section) that the wall is absolutely stable, though it runs up a steepish hill and also curves from start to finish.

(Bottom) **Nr Sennen, Cornwall,** 2 miles north-east of Land's End. 'Cyclopean' granite wall bounding a field and giving the impression that it is a natural outcrop put to use by an opportunist farmer.

(Top) **Nr Ambleside, Lake District.** This is an unusually attractive example of a Cumberland slate wall, for the gradations in the stone range from indigo, or near jet-black, through to palest grey and off-white. It happens to have been recently built, and fortunately the craftsmen made no attempt (as is so often done with multi-coloured bricks in suburban houses) to produce a set pattern within the limits of their material. They took each stone as it lay to hand, whether dark or light, provided it was of the right thickness for the course concerned, and laid it well and truly in position. The wall was then topped with slates set in cement but, unlike those in the preceding example, laid at an angle to the perpendicular reminiscent of the zigzag slate walling to be found throughout the slate districts of faraway Cornwall.

(Middle) **Nr Thorpe Cloud, Derbyshire.** This is characteristic dry-stone walling in the carboniferous limestone region. It is off-white or very pale grey, and weathers very little indeed. Thus a landscape criss-crossed by such walling as this—and there are hundreds of square miles of such landscape in Derbyshire north of Ashbourne, in the West Riding of Yorkshire, and further afield where the millstone-grit is less prevalent—produces an impression of tapestry. Moreover, there is a lightness, an airiness almost, about a landscape so criss-crossed that is not to be found where the more sombre and weathered millstone-grit predominates. It will be noted here that the cock-ups are not cement-set but balanced along the top of the uppermost course, and wedged together so expertly that they support one another against all the pressures of wind and weather and the hazards of clumsy scrambling feet.

(Bottom) **Nr Slack, West Riding of Yorkshire.** Millstone-grit quarries more easily than limestone, so it is possible to build a wall almost as uniform as (but infinitely more attractive than) one built of brick. This particular wall flanks a reservoir. It is evident that the men were instructed to make the wall unusually regular, which must have involved trimming and squaring the quarried stone. Yet there is surely just sufficient irregularity here to enable the wall to blend with the prevailing feature of the landscape of which it forms an integral part.

34

(Top left) **Guiting Power, Gloucestershire,** 5 miles west of Stow on the Wold, off B 4077. This is a characteristic Cotswold stile of a type designed to give pedestrians access to a footpath across a field, whether they are walkers making use of a right-of-way or the owner or a shepherd or other worker not requiring to use the gate. The protruding 'throughs' are massive blocks of the local oolitic limestone set in the wall in such a way that they offer a safe foothold on each side of the wall. Normally they are set so that the user ascends from left to right, and on the opposite side descends into the field from left to right. They are so proportioned that they are in equilibrium and do not disturb the set of the wall. The 'cock-ups' that run along the top of the wall are so massive and so skilfully set in place, shoulder to shoulder, that they are unlikely to be dislodged even by the clumsiest user.

(Top right) **Askrigg, Yorkshire, Wensleydale.** This 'squeeze-belly' stile is similar in pattern to the better-known example at Bibury, Gloucestershire, though being constructed of the local millstone-grit it presents a somewhat cruder appearance. Its low threshold has to be negotiated between close-set walls that make no concessions to a man's girth. The sides are rougher, less smoothed by time and use than those at Bibury. They certainly offer virtually no passage to the stray sheep or cow, which, of course, is the reason for the existence of this type of stile.

(Bottom left) **Nr Ambleside, Lake District.** This might be said to be a combination of the two types of stile—the 'throughs' in the wall, such as are used in the Cotswolds and in Yorkshire (and elsewhere), and the 'squeeze-belly' feature, though this one is little more than thigh-high. Nevertheless it would call for some dexterity in negotiating it—certainly in the half-light, or escaping from an irate bull!

(Bottom right) **Skenfrith, Monmouthshire,** 5 miles north-west of Monmouth, on B 4521. This is a somewhat crude version of the slate stile at Morwenstow, Cornwall—two low steps, and an edge-set slab that offers more than the minimum by way of obstacle to any but a fairly active and supple individual. Its most pleasing feature, perhaps, is the angle at which the side walls have been cut back to accommodate the main slab.

6. THATCH

Thatch—of reeds, straw, grass, leaves, turf or other natural material—is certainly the oldest form of roofing known to man. In England the great majority of thatched roofs are of barley, rye or wheat straw; but in regions where reed is grown, such as many parts of East Anglia and Somerset, this material is preferred. It is much more expensive than other thatching materials, and if a house-owner in some other part of the country wants a reed-thatched roof, he will have to pay the high cost of carriage on top of everything else. But a roof thatched with reed has a life at least twice, perhaps even three times, as long as even the best quality straw, so that once the initial cost has been met the owner need not consider further expense, probably for the rest of his life. However, precautions must be taken against birds right from the start —small-mesh wire netting expertly fitted over both thatch and eaves will do—otherwise the thatch will be penetrated; and once birds have started nesting, or foraging, in it there is little hope of getting rid of them, and the thatch, however good it is, is doomed to disintegrate.

Like dry-wallers, thatchers are a vanishing race of country craftsmen. Happily, there is evidence in districts where the craft has been indigenous that new blood is appearing. And the young men—as is demonstrated in new thatch recently seen in Shalbourne, Wiltshire—are showing the same aptitude and imagination as the veterans. Traditional designs peculiar to a region, a district, even to a parish, in the days when all but the Great Houses (even the churches) had roofs of thatch, have not wholly died out; at least, they are being resuscitated—to the delight of all who appreciate the continuance of an old tradition quite apart from the sheer beauty of a pattern which reveals the same individual touches long associated in a particular locality with one or other of the established thatcher families.

(Top) **Homersfield, Suffolk,** 5 miles south-west of Bungay, on B 1062. Almshouses in a 'model' village built round a trim garden with a thatched well-house in it.

(Bottom) **Wangford, Suffolk,** 3 miles north-west of Southwold, on A 12. Almshouses erected in 1931 by the 3rd Earl of Stradbroke, in memory of his fifteen-year-old son who died in Australia 'after a long illness bravely borne'.

(Top) **Private House, Yarcombe, Somerset,** 5 miles west of Chard, on A 30. This most attractive house stands near the foot of the notorious Yarcombe Hill, opposite the dog's-leg turn at its steepest part. It is a characteristic example of a West Country thatched residence of some standing: white-painted walls setting off the black paintwork of the window frames; smallish windows, lead-paned, only two of them on exactly the same level and of the same dimensions; and a porch with a thatched roof to match the roof that runs the full length of the house and slopes down at either end as though to enclose it wholly. The thatch is of straw, and gives the impression that before many more years have passed the time will have come to renew it. But the ornamental thatch along the roof-ridge and round the chimneys looks newer and certainly more artistic than the rest. A criss-cross pattern of spars has been laid on this uppermost area of thatch, and the lower edge, where it overlays the main thatch, is nicely scalloped, with a generous 'apron' descending below the chimney that divides the two halves of the roof.

(Bottom) **Public House, Leebotwood, Shropshire,** 3 miles north of Church Stretton, on A 49. In fact, it is something more than a mere public house. Modestly named the Pound Inn, its restaurant has a very high standard of cuisine. Its many gables, large and small, no two on the same level and no two identical, must have posed some problems for the thatcher employed to rethatch the roof not so long ago. The thatch, generally, is of immense thickness, and that over the porch is complicated by the fact that the doorway into the porch is not, as might be expected, beneath the gable but at the side, beneath a diminutive secondary roof of its own. The thatch here has been most cunningly contrived so that there is no weak spot for rain to penetrate. The angularity of the thatch over the four gables of varying proportions is nicely contrasted with the gentle sweeping curve of thatch over the wide doorway on the left of the building, which resembles a giant eyebrow slightly lifted in query or surprise.

(Top left) **Bredon, Worcestershire,** 3 miles north-east of Tewkesbury, on B 4080. A very trim example of a thatched limestone cottage (or pair of cottages) on the western fringe of the Cotswolds. The three gables—the centre one fractionally smaller than those flanking it— could be regarded, a little disrespectfully perhaps, as the Mad Hatter, the March Hare and the Dormouse from the tea table in **Alice in Wonderland;** the centre gable has that curious look of being sound asleep (like the Dormouse), the result, perhaps, of a 'blind' window set high up beneath the thatch. A modest attempt has been made here at topiary, but it is only a skeleton as yet.

(Top right) **Totnes, Devon,** 6 miles inland from Paignton. A particularly snug example of thatch on a cottage on the outskirts of this small town. The photograph was taken in the late afternoon, deliberately, so that the low sun could throw shadows that would accentuate the undulations of the thatch, here so shaped as to lie in a low curve over each of three small windows set high up beneath the eaves. There is an emphatic contrast between the pronounced curves of the main sweep of thatch and the slight pattern that runs parallel with the ridge-pole between the chimneys.

(Bottom left) **St Feock, Cornwall,** 5 miles south of Truro, off A 39. A cob cottage at the foot of the hill by which this 'lost' hamlet is reached, and just short of the church (and the seven-hole stocks p93). The cement-work up against the chimney is well in evidence—a thatched building costs a great deal to insure, and such precautions against fire **must** be taken. There is exceptionally bold thatch-patterning along the ridge-pole and dipping artistically below the chimney. The bird just visible towards the far end is not, this time, a thatcher's 'hallmark' but a chance visitor.

(Bottom right) **Nr Princes Risborough, Buckinghamshire,** 1 mile south, on A 4010. There is not a very great deal of thatch to be found in the Chilterns, though it cannot be called rare. This is a good example, showing several features not always in evidence. The thatch has been firmly pegged down along its extremities, though it is not held in position by weights, as it might be in Eire and the Western Isles; and there are three boldly marked 'patches', one over each gable and one below the chimney. The type of thatching is echoed in miniature over the neat little porch.

7. TOMBSTONES

'Of the writing of epitaphs there is no end,' as Bacon so nearly remarked; and, as Shakespeare so nearly observed, they are infinite in their variety. It might be thought that study of graveyard memorials is a morbid occupation. Far from it, however. For though a whole world of men may lie mouldering beneath the sod, their epitaphs, usually the inspiration of their bereaved families but sometimes their own work, make infinitely rewarding reading. With no more than a minuscule imagination you can weave stories and character studies about them that blend fiction with truth.

Who, and what, for instance, were the Carter sisters, Lucy and Christian, who were buried in old age a century and more ago in Kersey churchyard, Suffolk? Why did one of the sisters cause to be inscribed on their joint tombstone:

> Reader, pass on, nor waste thy time
> On bad biography, or bitter rhyme;
> For what I am, this humble dust enclose,
> And what I was—is no affair of yours.

Were they witches in their day, like the alleged witch at Seaton Ross, who wrote her own pathetic-challenging epitaph? Had they some murky secret, suspected but not proven by the Kersey folk, which produced this bitter quatrain? Yours is the solution.

Epitaphs can be grave or gay, enigmatic or forthright, sententious, deprecating, self-congratulatory, complacent, despairing, naive. They can be sincere, or wry comments on a life brought to untimely (or timely) end. They can move one to tears.

Upper Slaughter, Gloucestershire, 4 miles south-west of Stow-on-the-Wold, off A 436. There is no epitaph, not even a name, by which to identify the burial, only the date 1909. Few gravestones seen in any churchyard, however, have left so haunting a memory as this—in St Peter's, in a silent Cotswold village. A plaque in the church reads: 'This is a happy village. Though its men fought loyally in two World Wars, there were no deaths among them'. But there was a death here in 1909. The woman reclining on the grave has a Madonna-like cast of countenance that blends quietude with grief—for a loved one, no doubt, but perhaps expressing understanding of the griefs of those others whose loved ones lie here too.

(Top left) **Ashby St Mary, Norfolk,** 8 miles south-east of Norwich, off A 146. Ann Basey was manifestly a farmer's wife. Here she is, basket over her arm, feeding her brood of turkeys—for which Norfolk has been famed for centuries. Behind her, leaning over a fence, her husband watches her at her traditional task. She died almost exactly a hundred years ago. With her was buried her grandson Joseph, who died in infancy, as was so often the case in those days, especially in rural areas where doctors were rare and hygiene but little understood or practised.

(Top right) **Ashby St Mary, Norfolk.** The two tombstones stand close, side by side, by the path from gate to church porch. George Basey outlived his beloved wife by eight years. He was a sheep farmer, as the bas-relief shows us; but his (and her) turkeys are to be seen among the sheep. Buried with him are two grandsons, who also died in infancy. He tried so hard (as the tombstones make clear) to perpetuate the name Joseph; and was three times disappointed. It is what is **not** written that is so eloquent here.

(Bottom left) **Jevington, Sussex,** 3 miles west of Eastbourne, on B 2105. There is neither name nor date on this grave in the beautiful churchyard of St Andrew, but it is known to be that of a merchant shipowner whose vessels traded with China. So, the fine full-rigged three-master modelled in copper, now black (not green) with age, afloat on a granite slab with pennant flying from the foremast. A charming touch is the dinghy, also in copper, afloat beneath the vessel's counter, and attached by a fine cable. It is miraculous that this exquisite model has not been damaged or stolen.

(Bottom right) **Eyam, Derbyshire,** 5 miles north of Bakewell, on A 6010. Another tombstone that bespeaks its owner's main lifetime preoccupation. A cricketer for more than half his lifetime, both with his own county and with the MCC, one suspects that he 'ordered' his own tombstone and epitaph—perhaps even had the symbols inscribed on its highly polished base well in advance, knowing that he must reach his final over. Was his death a violent one? The crooked stumps, the scattered bails and deadly ball would suggest this. But his fellow-players leave one salient fact in no doubt whatever: he Played the Game, both literally and figuratively.

SACRED
TO THE MEMORY OF
ANN,
THE BELOVED WIFE OF
GEORGE BASEY,
WHO DIED 23RD JANRY 1868,
AGED 71 YEARS.
I SOUGHT THE LORD AND HE HEARD ME, AND DE
LIVERED ME FROM ALL MY FEARS.
ALSO OF
JOSEPH BASEY FISHER
WHO DIED 26TH JANY 1864,
IN HIS INFANCY.

SACRED
TO THE MEMORY OF
GEORGE BASEY,
WHO DIED 26 FEBY 1876,
AGED 82 YEARS.
THE LORD GAVE AND THE LORD HATH TAKEN AWAY,
BLESSED BE THE NAME OF THE LORD.
ALSO OF
JOSEPH BASEY FISHER,
WHO DIED IN HIS INFANCY 4TH JUNE 1873,
AND OF
JOSEPH BASEY FISHER,
AN INFANT WHO DIED 13TH SEP 1875.

TO
THE DEAR MEMORY OF
HARRY BAGSHAW
WHO DIED JANY 31ST 1927
AGED 67 YEARS.
FROM 1888 TO 1924 WITH
DERBYSHIRE & M.C.C.
WELL PLAYED.
FOR WHEN THE ONE GREAT SCORER COMES
TO WRITE AGAINST YOUR NAME,
HE WRITES — NOT THAT YOU WON OR LOST
BUT HOW YOU PLAYED THE GAME.

(Top left) **Blockley, Gloucestershire,** 3 miles south of Chipping Campden, on B 4479. Not, of course, in consecrated ground; actually, near the doorstep of an old-world cottage on the Dovedale side of this Cotswold village. The small stream in which, presumably, this long-lived and amiable trout spent its twenty happy and secluded years, flows past the cottage, which is appropriately named Fish Cottage.

(Top right) **Euston, Suffolk,** 3 miles south of Thetford, on A 1088. This odd tombstone is set in the wall surrounding Euston Park, and is one of two commemorating the death of well loved and faithful foxhounds. Trouncer was killed (it does not specify just how) in 1788. He is buried below this stone, whose inscription, surprisingly, is addressed to the fox: 'Foxes Rejoice; Here Buried Lies Your Foe'. One likes to think of the night-wandering vixen gazing up at these comforting words and going back to tell her husband and cubs the encouraging news.

(Bottom left) **Bampton, Devon,** 7 miles north of Tiverton, on A 396. Set low in the west wall of the tower of St Michael & All Angels church is this quaintly worded plaque commemorating the strange death of the Clerk's son, in 1776. It replaces the original plaque, which had become indecipherable. No one seems to know exactly how the Clerk's son died; presumably a pointed icicle hanging from high above fell and pierced the child's skull. The memorialist was less of a poet than a humorist. Nearby, at the foot of the tower, will be found the village stocks.

(Bottom right) **Stoke Poges, Buckinghamshire,** 5 miles south of Beaconsfield, on A 473. No 'storied urn or animated bust' this, even though it is in the churchyard that inspired Gray's **Elegy;** and no 'village Hampden, mute inglorious Milton, or Cromwell guiltless of his country's blood' occupies this grave. Beneath the stone lies 'Sandy', John Alexander McRae Collie, who died at the age of ten; and was buried, as were prehistoric chieftains (and others, more recently, in more primitive communities) with his possessions, in this case his favourite toys, which are displayed on the grave: his model yacht (with mainsail part-furled, symbolically) and his model locomotive. A ship's capstan and anchor suggest that the child had shared his father's interest in sailing.

(Top left) **Thursley, Surrey,** 3 miles north of Hindhead, off A 3. It stands in St Michael & All Angels churchyard, the tombstone of a young sailor brutally murdered near the Devil's Punchbowl, 2 miles to the south. There, an eroded memorial stone marks the actual spot, and incidentally names the three villains of the piece as Jas Marshall, Michael Gancy and Edw Lonegan 'who were all Taken on the Same Day and Hung in Chains Near This Place'. One wonders whether the official road-wideners of the A 3 suffered any penalty, for the stone also reads: 'Cursed be the Man who Injureth or Removeth This Stone'. The A 3 is, of course, the once-notorious Portsmouth Road.

(Top right) **Broadwey, Dorset,** 3 miles north of Weymouth, on A 354. Near the south porch of St Nicholas' Church, this tall stone carries a fine carving of a man's head, facing an equally notable carving of a girl's head. Artist and niece, face to face. 'Sacred to the memory of Thomas Henry Nicholson, Artist, a true, kind-hearted man of genius, 1815-1870. Also of Charlotte Neville, youngest child of his only sister, Mary Ann, 1858-1870.' And, almost illegible at the base of the stone: 'Her last words were—Suffer Me to Come to Thee'. A 'story', here, surely?

(Bottom left) **Morwenstow, Cornwall,** 5 miles north of Bude, off A 39. The **Caledonia,** from Arbroath, was wrecked off the cliffs in 1843, when the Rev Henry Hawker was vicar. The bodies of forty of the crew who were washed ashore were buried here, and over their mass grave Hawker placed the ship's figurehead, which also drifted ashore. The Scot brandishes a sword, and legend has it that if you risk walking too near it, at midnight, the sword will swing silently in the shadow and decapitate you!

(Bottom right) **Warden, Northumberland,** 2 miles north-west of Hexham. Beneath a great yew, in the churchyard of St Michael & All Angels, lie three graves, side by side, one smaller than the other two. All three graves are protected by a number of blacksmith-made wrought-iron hoops, installed with the aim of foiling body-snatchers, whose grisly trade a century or so ago was digging up corpses and selling them to unscrupulous anatomists for examination and experiment. The family of the Rev W. T. Shields were taking no chances with his corpse and those of his wife and eighteen-month-old child.

8. CHURCHYARD CROSSES

Tyberton, Herefordshire, 6 miles west of Hereford. This is a fine specimen of a medieval cross, almost certainly dating from the fourteenth century. It stands alongside the Church of St Mary, an eighteenth-century structure in the grounds of Tyberton Court, thus pre-dating it by some 400 years. It was so revered that when Cromwell came to power it was removed and buried underground, its precious 'gable-head' being hidden in the roof of the then church, to prevent its destruction. It was discovered only comparatively recently, and now a service is held annually at its base to commemorate its miraculous survival. As with many medieval crosses, it carries on one face, beneath the gable, a representation of the Crucifixion; the other face carries the customary representation of the Virgin and Child. Unusually, the Child Jesus is not sitting but standing, fully robed, on His Mother's knee. (There is another example of this at nearby Madley, also in Herefordshire.) The 10 ft shaft is beautifully tapered and octagonal in section, with delicate ornamentation at the point where it springs from its heavy plinth.

Gosforth, Cumberland. This is the tallest ancient cross in the country, standing more than 14 ft high. It dates back at least 900 years. The lower part of the shaft is cylindrical and elaborately portrays Yggdrasil, believed by the ancients to support the universe. Above this, the shaft is squared and carries the symbol of the Trinity on each face. The four faces carry a wealth of elaborate sculpturing, in which Dragons and Plaited Snakes, Odin, Loki and his wife Sigyn, the Horseman Surt, a Winged Dragon, Wolf and Hart, among other real and mythical creatures, are most intricately interwoven. There is evidence of strong Scandinavian influence here, and, since the cross is so ancient, it is certain that the carving was carried out by a craftsman steeped in Norse mythology. Nevertheless, as always, the Cross of Christ (somewhat unexpectedly in the Cornish tradition) dominates the whole. Considering its great age it is astonishing that this churchyard cross should be in such a remarkable state of preservation. Almost every detail of its elaborate pictorial mythology can be clearly picked out and understood.

Shaft, Alkborough, Lincolnshire, 6 miles north of Scunthorpe. Only six feet or so of the medieval churchyard cross survive to this day; the cross arms vanished, perhaps centuries ago. It possesses, however, one unique characteristic: though square in section, for most of its length it has 'weathered' in a most unusual fashion. In fact, this is not weathering at all, but the result of generations of weapon-sharpening. Here, down the centuries, soldiers and civilians alike have brought their cutting edges for honing on what must have proved excellent material; spearheads, swords, arrow-barbs, pikes, halberds, billhooks and sickles have all left their unmistakable marks on this cross shaft. It comes, therefore, into the category of **polissoirs,** along with those at Stokesay and Chedzoy, and the Roman water-trough at Housesteads. The shaft stands near the south porch of the ancient Church of St John the Baptist, which contains some fragments of Saxon work in the tower, since there was a church on this site before the Norman Conquest. The graveyard has 'risen' above the level of the approach-path by some 2 ft —the result, presumably, of the great number of burials over the centuries, which are said to number at least 8,000.

Crowcombe, Somerset, 4 miles south-east of Williton. This medieval cross is of the local and very pleasing russet-toned sandstone. It stands, as most such crosses do, near the south porch, and is 12 ft high, or very nearly, on a massive well worn plinth. Sculptured figures on the shaft represent John the Baptist; a mitred bishop holding his pastoral staff, his right hand raised in blessing; and a woman, traditionally believed to have been the Abbess of the twelfth-century Benedictine Nunnery at Studeley. All this is truly ancient, but the top of the cross is less so— a replacement following 'defacement by the puritanic ignorance of our ancestors', as a historian wrote some centuries ago. It is not easy to assess exactly what the top of the cross was intended to portray; but though it lacks the antiquity of the shaft that supports it, it certainly blends well with the intimate, mellow and picturesque quality of the setting which it graces.

(Left) **Bredon, Worcestershire,** 3 miles north-east of Tewkesbury, on B 4080. This elegant milestone stands isolated on a patch of turf at the entrance to this most attractive village of stone and thatch. (There is a similar milestone on the village green at Brampton, in Huntingdonshire, which possesses a set of beautifully incised hands.) Some 14 ft high, it is eye-catching indeed. There is nothing to indicate in which direction the various places named are to be found, but all happen to be near at hand: the most distant is only 12 miles away, the nearest less than a leisurely hour's walk. There is a soporific quality about this village. If you were rash enough to lie down on the apron of greensward round the obelisk, you might well fall asleep and, like Rip Van Winkle, sleep and sleep and sleep, to wake into another (and one hopes better) age. Even so, it is hard to believe that Bredon would be showing many signs of change after the sleep; there is an atmosphere of timelessness about it that is inescapable and most refreshing.

(Right) **Craven Arms, Shropshire,** $7\frac{1}{2}$ miles north-west of Ludlow, on A 49. This much older milestone stands 18 ft high and is perhaps most noteworthy for its slenderness and tapering sides. It marks the junction of the very busy Shrewsbury road with the B 4368 Clun road (on which stands the 2nd Lord Clive's beautiful direction-post at Little Brampton, a few miles to the west). On its three road-facing sides it carries thirty-six placenames and mileages, grouped in twelves. These range from Ludlow ($7\frac{1}{2}$ miles), by way of Manchester (91), Bath (97), Holyhead (136), London (150), Exeter (162), to Newcastle (223) and Edinburgh (295). The slender obelisk is highly vulnerable, standing where it does, for it was erected when traffic went at little more than walking pace, and its little white posts and linking chains offer no more than token protection. Though its upper part has obviously been broken off, and repaired, its base is intact; and this is a good thing, for the incised lettering is delicate and artistic enough to repay something more than a mere cursory passing glance.

Left obelisk:

1808

BREDON

UPTON
6 Miles.

PERSHORE
7 Miles.

EVESHAM
12 Miles.

TEWKESBURY
3 Miles.

WINCHCOMB
10 Miles.

CHELTENHAM
11 Miles.

Right obelisk:

	Miles		Miles
London	1?0	Edinburgh	
Oxford	91	Berwick	
Birmingham		Newcastle	28?
Plymouth	20?	York	1??
Portsmouth	16?	Manchester	
Exeter	16?	Burton	

Bath	97	Liverpool	79
Bristol	??	Chester	
Gloucester	6?		
Worcester			
Hereford			
Ludlow	7?		

The milestone, as has been noted, generally came later than the direction-post. In one sense, however, this is not strictly true, for the oldest known milestone in England is unquestionably the one near Bardon Mill in Northumberland, which was erected early in the second century AD by the builders of Hadrian's Wall. It stands there still, after eighteen centuries, a mile or so behind the Wall on the line of the Roman road, the Stangate, and is the only Roman milestone still standing where it was originally set up. There are, of course, many other, and more ornate, Roman milestones, often inscribed with the name of the emperor or district governor, to be found in various museums. But the milestone as we know it dates only from the Turnpike Acts of the second half of the eighteenth century. Unhappily, as road widening and straightening projects proliferate, more and more of these are being destroyed, replaced by the modern enamelled-iron pointers designed to help the speeding motorist. Many, too, were deliberately removed at the outbreak of World War II, and have never been replaced. If we eventually go over to the Continental kilometre-stone, the doom of the relatively small remainder will have been finally sealed.

Esher, Surrey. Most milestones are unimpressive, in stone (square or triangular), or cast iron (triangular, flat or cylindrical); but, as with direction-posts, there are a few that stand out as giants—original, impressive, sometimes even startling. This one, known as 'The White Lady of Esher' (it must once have been white, but today is sombre grey save for the plinth and ball), stands outside the Orleans Arms just north of the town. Nearly 10 ft high and 3 ft thick, it bears the date 1767. In fact, it was erected earlier in that century by the Duke of Newcastle, sometime Secretary of State in George II's reign, who owned a private estate near Esher, and erected this pretentious 'milestone' to enable Court and Parliamentary couriers (and occasionally the Royal coach) to find the estate when he was in residence. The pillar carries a round score of placenames, with relevant mileages. The shortest, 1 mile, was to his estate, the longest to Portsmouth, 57 miles distant, down the notorious Portsmouth Road, now the A 3.

(Top left) **Nr Horsebridge, Sussex,** 12 miles north of Eastbourne, on A 22. This is a particularly well preserved example of the 'rebus' or 'puzzle' milestone. A number of them are still to be seen on the main London to Eastbourne road, especially on the south-east section running from East Grinstead and Forest Row. The figure, of course, denotes the mileage from London; the little bow and pendant of three or more bells is a pictograph for 'Bow Bells'—the point in London from which a number of southbound roads officially started. The 'stones' are in fact cast-iron plates affixed either to stones or, more rarely, to wooden blocks.

(Top right) **Cambridge,** on A 10. Just south of Cambridge. This is the first of a series of 'Trinity' milestones set up by the Master of Trinity College in 1728, thus maintaining a tradition started a century and more earlier when a royal bequest of £1,000 was designated for the marking and measuring of this important main road. Like all of them, it bears the crescent and rings within an ornamental shield, closely associated, of course, with the ancient foundation of the college. These milestones may be seen along the road southwards in the direction of Royston, in the next county.

(Bottom left) **Sturry, Kent,** 3 miles north-east of Canterbury, on A 28. It stands immediately outside the Swan Inn, in the middle of the pavement. Originally the road into Thanet passed the front of the inn (this is now bypassed by 100 yd or so), when the main traffic was horse-drawn and horse-borne—wagons and bagmen. The ring set in the top of this small stone was used for tethering the horses, while their owners slipped inside for a little light refreshment.

(Bottom right) **Nr Callington, Cornwall,** off the A 390 Liskeard road. The old coach road climbed steeply from the tollgate at the Lynher bridge. An additional horse (at an additional charge) was hitched on to coach or wagon, to take it to the top of the hill. There it was unhitched and led back to the toll house, a mile or so away. The official point at which this obligatory extra horse-power might be dispensed with was at the gate of a farm, marked by this crudely inscribed 'Take Off' stone. There are several other such stones on these old routes, though most of them are now lost.

10. ROCK MONSTERS

Vixen Tor, Dartmoor, Devon, 5 miles east of Tavistock. The 'tors'—
—a variant of 'towers'—of Dartmoor are among the most spectacular
features of the country. They are not peculiar to Dartmoor, for they
appear also on Bodmin Moor, to the west; but the most numerous, as
well as the most imposing, of them are all to be found there. Dartmoor,
of course, is granite country. Experts state that in remote geological
times this part of England was one vast sheet of granite rising to many
thousands of feet above its present height above sea level. Hard as this
stone is, however, it has been eroded away by millions of years of
weather of varying types and severity to what remains to be seen today.
Dartmoor itself covers some 250 square miles (Bodmin Moor is considerably smaller); and for the most part you are not conscious of the
granite of which it is composed, since this is almost entirely covered by
a thick skin of shaggy turf.

Nevertheless, you cannot travel far across it before being impres-
sively reminded of the skeleton beneath that skin, for some of the
granite has been more resistant to erosion than the rest, and it is this
granite that survives above the surface, in the form of the tors. In all
there are not far short of 200 of these, ranging from giants known to
every visitor to the Moor down to the modest outcrops that you could
find only if you went in search of them with a large-scale map. Among
the giants are the well known Hay Tor, Great Mis Tor and Hound Tor.
To these you might add Hessary and Bagga, Sittaford and Manaton,
Sheeps and Beardown; and, most certainly, Vixen Tor.

This tor, though unlike most tors it stands in a hollow rather than on
a height, is in fact the highest rock-mass on Dartmoor, rising nearly
100 ft on its steepest side. Its name is most inappropriate, even incongruous. A more suitable one would have been 'Sphinx'; even 'Lion'
would have been more apt. Still, rightly named or not, it presents from
all aspects a magnificent spectacle of granite-in-ruin: the original solid
block has shattered along its cleavage-lines until it looks as though it
has been sculptured **in situ** by some primeval giant with a hammer that
the god Thor might have wielded and a chisel to match.

The Bowder Stone, Borrowdale, Cumberland, 5 miles south of Keswick. In addition to the granite tors of Dartmoor and Bodmin Moor, the gritstone masses such as the Norber Rock 'erratics' near Austwick, in Yorkshire, and the Brimham Rocks elsewhere in the same county, England has a great number of isolated rocks that stand out in spectacular fashion from the landscape and thus over the centuries have acquired nicknames. One such is the Devil's Chimney, near Leckhampton in Gloucestershire. There are sea-cliff 'stacks', such as those off the Dorset and Devon coasts. There are 'logan-stones', or rocking stones, such as that on the headland near Treen, close to Land's End— so finely balanced that it can be set in motion by the pressure of one hand. Indeed, a century and more ago it was tipped off balance entirely, and its recovery and rebalancing involved a whole army of men.

The largest single stone, bar none, however, is the Bowder Stone— 'bowder', of course, being a North Country variant of 'boulder'. It is to be found in what is almost universally acknowledged to be the most beautiful valley in the Lake District, though it is easy enough to miss if you do not know where to look for it, huge as it is. Just beyond the hamlet of Grange-in-Borrowdale, a steepish track climbs away to the left of the road, through close-set trees, for a quarter of a mile or so. It will lead you straight to this gigantic boulder, a giant to dwarf all others that you may have seen. Roughly a cube in shape, it is some 50 ft across and about the same in height. Experts have assessed its weight as little short of 2,000 tons. The really remarkable thing about the Bowder Stone, apart from its huge size, is the fact that it is balanced securely on one corner poised on a rock ledge. Its 'foot' is so small that two people lying on the turf facing one another can without difficulty clasp each other's hands round it. Yet it is absolutely rigid, and a dozen or more people can comfortably stand on the top, which is reached by wooden steps.

Unlike the Norber 'erratics' this boulder was not brought to the site by a retreating ice-sheet; it is in fact a block of native metamorphic rock that broke away from the cliff face behind it and, by a freak of chance equilibrium, remained firmly poised on one corner just as you see it today.

66

'The Dancing Bear', Brimham Rocks, Yorkshire, south-east of Pateley Bridge. On a plateau of millstone-grit nearly 1,000 ft above sea level there extends over some 60 acres an extraordinary assembly of grit-stone outcrops, wind-eroded over the aeons into the most fantastic shapes. Many of the individual masses are strange enough to have acquired singularly appropriate nicknames. Perhaps the most outstanding of these is the so-called Dancing Bear, beloved of every child who comes exploring here. But there are other rock masses only just less singular: the Devil's Anvil, for example; the Druids' Altar (with its echo of Stonehenge and other prehistoric sites); the Pulpit (perhaps as a challenge to the presence of the Devil); the Idol Rock (back to paganism again); the Tortoise, the Rabbit and the Rhinoceros; and, perhaps a little far-fetched, though it is wonderful what a pattern of sunlight and shadow can do to persuade the willing beholder, the Yoke of Oxen. In remote ages Brimham Rocks was a solid plateau of millstone-grit and carboniferous limestone; what confronts you today is the result of many millions of years of erosion by wind and weather.

'Bowerman's Nose', Dartmoor, Devon, 4 miles south of Moretonhampstead. Too small to rank among the many 'tors' of Dartmoor, this extraordinarily lifelike granite stack is notable in its own right, and well worth the tortuous journey to locate it. The stack is, of course, an outcrop from the original huge granite 'dome' that covered so much of Devonshire and Cornwall; where the rest of the granite has been eroded, this rock mass has survived. It rises to only 20 ft or so, but because the ground falls away beneath it on three of its four sides it gives the impression of being much higher than it is. It completely dominates the low-lying ground to the north. Local tradition holds that this pseudo-tor was named after a recluse named Bowerman who made his abode among the tumbled boulders of Hound Tor, a few miles to the south. Whether or not this is true, this granite mass, split into blocks of varying size and poised on a steepish slope set about with lesser outcrops and patches of treacherous marshy ground, certainly bears some sort of a likeness to, let us say, Neanderthal Man.

11. BUILDINGS

Oast-houses. It is true that you will find the oast-house in Herefordshire and Worcestershire, but it flowers in its greatest glory and profusion in Kent, where hops have been grown for the making of beer for more than 400 years. The hop-drying kilns, with their attendant chambers, known as oasts, have been the predominant feature of this county, particularly the region known as the Weald, running eastwards from Tonbridge, for almost all that time, though few of the surviving oasthouses were built earlier than the eighteenth century. How many of them there are today it would defeat any Kentish man, or Man of Kent (traditionally distinguished), to estimate; but hundreds, most certainly. For beer is still our national beverage, and where beer is brewed hops must be grown in hop-gardens (in the West Country they are called hop-fields), and be meticulously kiln-dried.

You will have noticed that oast-houses can be square or round. The earliest oasts were built square, in the sixteenth century, but the majority, perhaps all, of these have now vanished, though the tradition was maintained in later building. The round ones date mainly from the mid-eighteenth century and later, and therefore are the most numerous. But, square or round, they conform to a regular basic pattern. They are brick-built, between 16 and 20 ft in diameter, and surmounted by a tapering tiled roof (cone- or pyramid-shaped) which in turn is surmounted by the cowl and vane necessary to promote draught and, in gusty weather, to prevent down-draught.

They may stand singly, in twos and threes and fours, or in batteries, according to whether they belong to some small operator or to some large industrial combine such as one of the great brewers. But whether in ones or in half-dozens, they are immediately eye-catching, both at a distance and near at hand, and amply reward the photographer who is prepared to wait for the sun and roving cloud to offer him a variety of atmosphere in his pictures. (They have this in common with windmills.) Oast-houses have widely attracted the home-maker, who has been quick to snap up any abandoned house, restore it and adapt it to his own needs. (Again, they have this in common with windmills.)

If you are fortunate enough to be invited to enter a working oast, do not hesitate, for this is a rural industry that has few parallels anywhere in the country. On the ground floor of the oast there stands a raised fireplace on which a fire, usually of smokeless fuel like anthracite, burns, with a pan of sulphur alongside to preserve the hops from mildew

spores. Some 20 ft above your head there is a floor of slats, covered with fine netting, horsehair or burlap. Spread over this to the depth of a foot or so will be hops, evenly raked across, and weighing perhaps as much as a ton. Hops must be dried slowly, consistently, for a period of anything from eight to twenty-four hours, according to their condition when picked. The attendant, a veteran of many years of hop-drying, skilled and dedicated, will remain throughout the period, however long, tending the fire, checking the temperature, calculating the dryness or otherwise of the hops, never leaving them until the optimum state has been achieved.

(Previous page) **Oast-houses, Sissinghurst Castle, Kent,** 3 miles north-east of Cranbrook, off A 262. These are in the grounds of what was until recently the home of Sir Harold Nicolson and Vita Sackville-West, writer and gardener-extraordinary. It is now National Trust property. This fine battery of square oasts is close to the magnificent Gate House.

(Top left) **Oast-houses nr Headcorn, Kent,** 10 miles south-east of Maidstone, off B 2078. A pair of oasts attached to a tiled and weather-boarded dwelling, overlooking a still pond framed by pollarded willows. A scene perhaps peculiar to Kent, but easy to match over and again in this matchless county, 'The Garden of England'.

(Top right) **Oast-houses nr Goudhurst, Kent,** off A 262, 12 miles south of Maidstone. A perfect example of the impression of serenity induced by the relationship—companionship, even—of oast and dwelling-house, russet-brown and white paint, in an orchard setting—as can be recognised from the fruit-picker's ladder.

(Bottom) **Oast-houses at Beltring, Kent,** 5 miles east of Tonbridge, on B 2015. Mass-production, assembly-line hop-drying in the true heart of oast-house country, within a mile or so of Yalding, its traditionally accepted focal point. Less picturesque, admittedly, than the others, the 'little-uns'; but it conveys admirably the impression of what hops mean to Kent, and have meant for four long centuries.

(Top) **The Gate House, Great Chart, Kent,** 2 miles west of Ashford, on A 28. It stands by the roadside at the corner of the churchyard of St Mary the Virgin, on the brow of a hill rising westwards from the village. During the five centuries of its life it has been known as the Priest's House, the Church Gate House, and the Pest House. A plaque on the wall gives it this name today, but the so-called Pest Houses date from the Great Plague of 1665, a century and a half later than the date when this house was built. It is half-timbered, with plasterwork in-filling and a heavy tiled roof whose eaves cast deep shadows over the diamond-paned windows. The far end, with the chimney, is of brickwork, incorporated in the churchyard wall and so knitting church and gatehouse into one entity. It was probably designed originally for the rector or chantry priest, but it has been used in turn by pilgrims to Canterbury, 16 miles to the east, by a succession of churchwardens for their official business meetings, held today in Church Halls, and as accommodation for generations of vergers and sextons. Most recently it has served as the Sunday School for this most delightful village.

(Bottom) **The Cat House, Henfield, Sussex,** 12 miles north-west of Brighton, on A 281. This sixteenth-century thatched and half-timbered cottage is to be found at the foot of the lane leading up to the church. Its unusual feature is the frieze of cat silhouettes beneath the ornate thatched eaves. It is said that the cottage was formerly occupied by an elderly canary-loving eccentric, and the vicar, who had to pass close by on his way to the church, was always accompanied by his cat. One day his cat killed the elderly lady's canary. As a reprisal, she hung a metal effigy of a cat beneath the eaves, where the vicar must inevitably both hear and see it, and be mortified by the reminder that a priest's cat had killed a parishioner's canary. Eventually, however, the old lady died, the cottage became someone else's property, the cat-effigy was dismantled, and the feud became a thing of the past. But village traditions die hard, and the new owner had to bow to public opinion, and keep the story on record in visual form. Hence the array of cats in the plaster panels between the oak beams, each with a canary held in its forepaws!

(Top) **Round Houses, Veryan, Cornwall,** 8 miles south-east of Truro, off A 3078. When you enter this tiny hamlet from the north, you are immediately confronted by the Round House (top left), with thatched roof, thatched porch, shell-encrusted windows, and a simple cross surmounting all. The southern exit, at the top of a steep narrow hill, is marked by a pair of similar Round Houses, one on either side (top right shows one). A wall, as well as the windows overlooking the road, is encrusted with ornamental shells. Around the irregular perimeter of the hamlet are yet more Round Houses, all differing in detail but fundamentally the same. Cornishmen are both superstitious and religious (a distinction not always easy to draw), and all the Round Houses have one feature in common—each is surmounted by a simple cross. (One of them is sadly awry!) The crosses were warnings to the Devil, of whose power the villagers (or at least their forefathers) were acutely conscious. The proliferation of the Round Houses was deliberate: His Hellish Majesty, it was firmly believed, would be obliged to spend so much time trying to make up his mind which way to pounce that, with luck (or God's blessing), the villagers might hope to escape his attentions altogether!

(Bottom left) **Culbone Church, Somerset,** 5 miles west of Porlock, off A 39. It is easy to accept the claim that this is England's smallest church —35 ft long, it can just seat thirty people on its cramped pews. Walls and south porch are twelfth-century; the tiny truncated spire somewhat later. It has an interesting two-light window to the chancel, of which frame, mullion and transom are carved out of a solid square of sandstone. To reach the church involves a long hard scramble through stunted trees and thick scrub down a steep and treacherous combe.

(Bottom right) **Belfry, Pembridge, Herefordshire,** 5 miles east of Kington, on A 44. This detached belfry (reminiscent of that at Brookland, Kent, though further removed from its church) is a massive structure of enormous oak timbers mounted inside a stone enclosing wall and supporting a steeply pitched roof which itself carries a second structure with its own roof and tiled turret. A fine peal of bells is grouped amid the treetrunk-like framing, together with the works of the clock, which is curiously offset below the turret, and was installed in 1889 by the widow of the Rev Crouch, who had been rector there for some forty years.

The Round Tower is primarily associated with the Irish scene. Known as **clochteachs**—pencil-thin towers rising to 100 ft or so—they proliferate in Galway, Louth, Fermanagh, Neath, Waterford and elsewhere, the most outstanding being perhaps the Rattoo, and those of Ardmore and Glendalough. There are somewhat similar towers in Orkney, where they are called **brochs.** In England they belong essentially to East Anglia, and especially to Norfolk and Suffolk.

Like the **clochteachs,** they were built primarily as lookout towers and for security, in the tenth and eleventh centuries, against the Vikings and later Norse invaders who ran their longships up the estuaries from the North Sea, the rivers then being navigable for many miles of their winding length inland. But unlike **clochteach** or **broch,** they are built of flint—for there is little other stone in East Anglia suitable for building (though suitable stone was indeed found for building the magnificent 'wool' churches, such as those of Lavenham, Kersey and Stoke-by-Nayland).

Because stone generally was lacking to form the quoins necessary for the angles of square-built towers, these had to be built in the round. Local flint, bonded in cement, was the material also used by the Romans at Burgh Castle, centuries earlier. The use of flint involved building, not course by course as with brick or stone, but 'spirally', as in primitive basket-making, a method excellently demonstrated in the famous Round Tower at Wortham.

Church of St Mary the Virgin, Wortham, Suffolk, 4 miles west of Diss, on A 143 Gt Yarmouth road. The tower overlooks the River Waveney, which here divides Suffolk from Norfolk and afforded the Vikings easy access to the interior. Across the green from the inn, named Tumble-down-Dick to commemorate the fall of Richard Cromwell, looms this enormous tower through the trees. Some 60 ft in height and 100 ft in girth, its circular wall is a yard thick at the base and towers above the west end of the church. Formerly, of course, it was higher still. The existing portion gives the curious impression of being 'telescopic', in that each section upwards is slightly less in diameter than the one supporting it.

(Top left) **St Mary's Church, Haddiscoe, Norfolk,** 5 miles north of Beccles, on A 143. The church dominates the shallow valley eastwards to the coastline between Lowestoft and Great Yarmouth. The 60 ft tower was built as a lookout well before the Norman Conquest. Its wall is so thick that when, five centuries later, bells were installed, a spiral staircase was carved out of it. The top section, of knapped-flint squares, was added several centuries after the original building. Below it, the door of the south porch has wrought ironwork believed to have been made by a blacksmith influenced by the Viking tradition. It may be compared with that of Stillingfleet church.

(Top right) **St Peter's Church, Theberton, Suffolk,** 7 miles north of Aldeburgh, on B 1122. Its unusually long nave is thatched, and its flint tower is capped by a somewhat later octagonal section that merges easily with the round. Parts of the church are early Norman. In its south porch is a macabre memorial—a fragment from a Zeppelin commemorating the burial in the churchyard of its crew. Near the gate stands a rusted Gatling gun inscribed to the effect that, though it commemorates the brave men of Theberton who gave their lives for others in World War I, it should remind us today that 'it is a better thing to walk in the Paths of Peace'.

(Bottom left) **Church of the Most Holy Trinity, Barsham, Suffolk,** 3 miles west of Beccles, on A 1116. An unusually attractive carved lych-gate (see p 21), reached by a track across a cow pasture, gives access to this beautiful ancient church of flint and thatch set among trees. Its round tower is nearly 60ft in height, the lower half Saxon, the upper and narrower portion Norman. Adjacent is an unusually fine rectory, with a portico.

(Bottom right) **St Andrew's Church, Little Snoring, Norfolk,** 4 miles north-east of Fakenham, just north of the A 148 Cromer road. This church is unusual in that its modest round tower stands a foot or two clear of and detached from the main fabric. It is built almost entirely of locally quarried flint, but has a few courses of rough-hewn stone at shoulder height, and is 'stepped' halfway up. It is capped by a charming cone roof and finial, from which four diminutive dormer windows gaze outwards. Its first rector was inducted in 1292.

(Top left) **The Huer's House, Newquay, Cornwall.** This near-circular building, with an outside stairway to the uneven roof, is a reminder of the seaside resort's one-time importance as a base for a fishing-fleet. It was from the harbour immediately below the promontory on which it stands that the pilchard boats sailed out beyond Towan Head into the Atlantic, and they sailed only when the official 'Huer', permanently on lookout here, spyglass to eye, located the great pilchard shoals and summoned the men to their boats. Its thick slate walls are pierced with diamond-shaped unglazed windows, looking over the water to distant Trevose Head.

(Top right) **Hawker's Hut, Morwenstow, Cornwall,** 6 miles north of Bude, off A 39. This must surely be the smallest and crudest of all the National Trust properties! It is to be found at the top of a 500 ft cliff half a mile due west of the Church of St Morwenna, of which the Rev Robert Stephen Hawker was vicar for forty years until 1875. He constructed the Hut himself, largely out of salvaged driftwood, as a place of retreat where, looking out over an inspiring cliff- and sea-scape, he could meditate and write the poems for which he is still loved and remembered.

(Bottom left) **Ye Olde Coffin House, Brixham, Devon,** 8 miles south of Torquay. The improbable story behind this strange building close to the picturesque harbour is that a Brixham ship's chandler told his daughter's suitor that he would rather see her in her coffin than married to him. The suitor, however, was imaginative as well as determined. He employed a builder to construct a house to the rough proportions of a coffin. So impressed was the prospective father-in-law that he relented; the couple were duly married and, of course, lived there happily ever after.

(Bottom right) **House-in-the-Cliff, Porthcurno, Cornwall,** 3 miles south-east of Land's End. This 'one-up-one-down' house is not so much built as squeezed into a cleft in the huge cliff that soars above Porthcurno Bay and carries the road steeply westwards to the Minack Theatre and Land's End itself, just beyond. Stone steps arch over a rock 'basement' and lead to a narrow door in keeping with the strait-ened proportions of the house, with one window alongside and another immediately above. The view out to sea takes in the promontory bear-ing the famous Treen logan-stone.

Gannymede Model Village, Hastings, Sussex. The scale of this most originally conceived miniature village, occupying half an acre of clifftop outside the town, is 1 in to 1 ft. Because, almost unbelievably, every one of the many and variegated buildings here is the work of one man, the artist-craftsman who designed and built it, Gannymede offers a stronger impression than most of careful integration. Furthermore, it is 'growing' all the time. It took some three years to build enough of it to be formally opened (by the Mayor of Hastings) some fifteen years ago; regular visitors are quick to notice that there is always something new to be seen since their previous visits.

One feature of special interest here is the extent to which the site has been landscaped-in-miniature and filled with dwarf plants to maintain the scale. The parish church spire rises to twice the height of a small boy; a spacious and mellowed manor house stands on the outskirts; the shops are owned by 'Briskett the Butcher' and 'Q.Cumber the Greengrocer', and so on. (You may wince at the puns, but Gannymede was designed for the delectation of children, whose tastes in this respect are simpler than those of their elders!) Tangbourne Abbey, alas, is in ruins; but Tangbourne Church and the almshouses flourish. So too does the home farm. The walls of Gannymede Castle stand proudly, as they have done (you are to suppose) for centuries, perhaps since the coming of William the Conqueror, who fought King Harold at the Battle of Hastings only a few miles from this site in 1066.

The true country scene is well represented by scale-model oasthouses; weather-boarded mills have their mill-wheels turning in running water, for a stream flows through the village, with goldfish swimming in it. There is a windmill, too, once a familiar feature in south-east England, and a miniature public school, King's College; on a fine summer's day its playing fields are filled with miniature cricketers in play. It seems likely that this village will soon have outgrown its site on the clifftop, since the inexhaustible flow of ideas from its imaginative and original creator are causing it almost literally to burst at the seams. This is indeed a little world in artistic microcosm, with a new small delight at every other turn.

12. MISCELLANY

Messiter's Cone, Barwick, Somerset, 2 miles south of Yeovil. Scattered about a stretch of parkland just off the A 37 Yeovil to Dorchester road, near a hamlet locally pronounced 'Barrick', is a quartet of very oddly shaped buildings indeed. They serve no useful purpose today; but in the early years of the last century their erection by the philanthropically minded George Messiter gave employment to a number of men whose trade, that of glove-making, had come to an end.

It is not on record who was actually responsible for the design of these weird structures; not surprisingly, they have acquired nicknames in the century and a half and more during which they have stood here. One of them consists of a rough stone arch supporting a cylindrical column, from whose top springs lightly into the air a graceful representation of Hermes, messenger of the gods, somewhat reminiscent of Piccadilly's Eros—though it bears the unexpected nickname of 'Jack-the-Treacle-Eater'. The story goes that it commemorates a youthful employee of Messiter who made regular journeys to London and back, on foot, and trained on treacle. There are Barwick folk who still believe that if a basin of treacle is left by it at night, Hermes-Jack will have descended and swallowed it by morning and licked the basin clean. Another of the quartet is known as the 'Fish Tower', so named because it originally carried a large weathervane in the shape of a fish. Unfortunately the weathervane, and the lantern that carried it, have long since vanished.

The most elegant of the quartet by far is the one shown opposite. It stands remote from the other three, as though conscious of its superiority over its fellows. Four gracefully proportioned Gothic-type arches support a beautifully tapered cone, pierced by a large number of square orifices. The smooth uppermost courses of this mainly rough-hewn stonework are surmounted by a stone sphere, 75 ft from the ground. The cone better deserves the nickname 'The Needle' than does the one that actually bears that name, for it has the slimness of the slimmest of church spires. Though most of its stone structure is rough-hewn, the overall effect is of grace and elegance. Considering it is the work of wholly unskilled men, the fact that it has stood for well over a century and a half, and is still in good shape, is as remarkable as is its design and execution.

Memorial to Maud Heath. Maud Heath was a public-spirited woman who left her mark in her native Wiltshire almost exactly 500 years ago, in 1474. She is recalled in statue form on top of a column in a field at Monument Farm on the crest of Wick Hill, some 4-5 miles east of Chippenham. There she sits, a buxom countrywoman, with a basket of eggs and poultry hanging over her left arm. A farmer's wife, she sold her produce in the market at Chippenham, one of the old market towns and, to reach it, she had to cross the wide and shallow valley of the Avon, which was all too often flooded in autumn, winter and spring. Having made sufficient money, she selflessly devoted it to the construction of a brick-and-stone causeway carried on nearly seventy small arches. She and her neighbours were thus enabled to cross the level water-meadows dry-shod even when they were flooded to a depth of several feet. The causeway is there to this day, still used by pedestrians passing from Wick Hill to Langley Burrell, where its builder died a widow nearly 500 years ago.

At the eastern end of the causeway a stone obelisk was erected in 1698 by the trustees of the fund she providently left in her will for the upkeep of the causeway. The obelisk carries an inscription recording her munificence. Beneath the globe which surmounts the whole are four sundials, of which, of course, only the southward-facing one is effective. Beneath the sundials are inscriptions designed to make the passer-by reflect upon the transitoriness of life and the advisability of obeying God's Laws:

> Life steals away this Hour, O Man, is lent Thee;
> Patiently work the work of Him Who sent Thee!

and:

> Haste, Traveller! The sun is sinking now;
> He shall return again—but never Thou!

and again:

> Oh Early Passenger, look up, be Wise,
> And think how, night and day, Time onward flies!

A final message to the 'passenger', or passer-by reads: 'Injure Me Not'.

To the memory
of the worthy MAUD
HEATH of Langly Bur-
rell Widow.
   Who in the year
of Grace 1474 for the
good of Travellers did in
Charity bestow in Land
and houses about Eight
pounds a year forever, to
be laid out on the High
ways and Cauſey lead-
ing from Wick Hill to
Chippenham Clift.

   This Piller was
ſet up by the feoffees in
1698.

Injure me not.

Cider-mills. Cider-making is largely concentrated in the West Country, short of Cornwall and west Devon; that is to say, in parts of Somerset, Herefordshire and Worcestershire. The symbol of the industry, which this area of England shares with Normandy, is the cider-mill and cider-press; a community with a long tradition takes pride in displaying the symbols of its occupation, and nowhere is this more true than in this cider region.

Cider-making involves two basic processes. The first is the initial crushing of the cider apple in the cider-mill; the second is the squeezing of the crushed apple in the press, a somewhat crude piece of apparatus having much in common with the cheese presses of Wensleydale and elsewhere. The cider-mill, being more substantially constructed of materials less likely to deteriorate, such as granite, is more often to be seen than the cider-press; there is, however, a good specimen of the latter at Mortimer's Cross in Herefordshire.

The cider-mill consists of a circular stone trough in which one, or sometimes two, stone wheels rotate, actuated by means of a central spindle kept in motion by a horse walking round a stone platform outside the trough and harnessed to the wheels through a linkage of oak beams and iron brackets. Formerly an ox, or a bullock, was employed, as is still the case in many countries bordering on the Mediterranean, where water must be drawn up from wells for distribution through irrigation channels. The wheels, usually of granite, are bevelled so that they make good contact with the stone.

(Top) **Hereford,** on the eastern outskirts of the town, beside the Bromyard road, A 465. This is a particularly well preserved specimen of a single-stone cider-mill, erected in the grounds of the newly established Churchill Museum of local crafts. The bevel on the granite stone is clean-cut, probably done since its installation on the new site.

(Bottom) **Cheltenham,** on the southern outskirts of the town, beside the Oxford road, A 40. This is private property—a gesture by someone who appreciates local tradition, even though the house lies somewhat outside the true cider region. Note how worn the bevelled edges of the stone have become, with generations of use. Note, too, the wrought-iron bracket to which the animal's harness would have been attached.

Stocks have provided a simple and effective means of minor punishment-on-the-spot for wrongdoers for more than 600 years and remained in general use until perhaps a century and a half ago. They were—and often still are—to be found on village greens, outside churches, by village lock-ups, or anywhere where the occupant could be kept under observation and was at the mercy of the unsympathetic passer-by with a ripe tomato or rotten egg to throw. Incorporated with the stocks very often was a whipping-post, at which the wrongdoer was flogged before being set to cool his heels in the stocks below. There might also be a pillory adjacent, for use at need.

There are good examples of stocks at Little Budworth, Cheshire; at Ripley, Yorkshire; at Aldbury, Hertfordshire, complete with whipping-post; and at Ninfield, Sussex, where stocks and whipping-post are unusual in that they are a blacksmith's handiwork, not an assembly of heavy timbers, as at Abinger Common, Surrey, and elsewhere. For every example cited up and down the country, a score and more could be mentioned.

(Top) **Colne, Lancashire.** This set of stocks is rare, probably unique in the country, in that it is mounted on wheels. It now stands among the graves surrounding the Parish Church of St Bartholomew, beneath a tiled lych-gate-type roof. Why the wheels? Were they to enable the stocks to be brought to the scene of the crime? Were they wheeled with the occupant installed? This set of stocks, unusually, has a hinged oak back rest. Was Authority so solicitous for the occupant's comfort, then? It will be noted that the three pairs of holes are set very close together; fully occupied, this set of stocks, for all its wheels and back-rest, must have been extraordinarily uncomfortable.

(Bottom) **St Feock, Cornwall,** 5 miles south of Truro, off A 39. Here and there you will come across a set of stocks in which there is an odd number of holes. One stands beneath the Butter Cross in Oakham, Rutland. Another, with seven holes this time, is to be found in the porch of the little Parish Church of St Feock, in a remote corner of the Duchy of Cornwall. You will find that, however hard you try to 'pair' the holes, no two adjacent ones are of the same diameter. It seems that the customary occupants, the vagrants and sturdy vagabonds of the district, were very oddly legged!

92

Whetstones for arrows and spears—technically known as **polissoirs**—are to be found wherever there is suitable stone for the purpose. They may be random sarsens, or hewn stone, as at Housesteads on Hadrian's Wall; they may be quoins in the corners of churches or barns; they may be the shafts of church crosses—there is an outstanding example of this in the churchyard at Alkborough, Lincolnshire (p 55). They may even be gravestones that happened to possess just the right quality of texture and grain.

(Top left) **Stokesay Castle, Shropshire,** 5 miles north-west of Ludlow, off A 49. The uprights framing the tombstone of Alice and Henry Baugh, who died in the mid-seventeenth century, are characterised by a number of vertical clefts, narrow and deep, in which arrowheads were sharpened; and by a number of smooth concave curves in which spearheads and swords were honed to a fine cutting edge.

(Top right) **Chedzoy, Somerset,** 3 miles east of Bridgwater, off A 39. These **polissoirs** (of both types) are to be found on the corner of the buttress against the south transept of the Church of St Mary the Virgin. They are believed to have been made by Monmouth's rebel soldiery, who had to arm themselves with makeshift weapons, such as sickles and billhooks as well as spears, for use in the Battle of Sedgemoor, which was fought in 1685 barely more than 2 miles south of this church.

(Bottom left) **Stratton, Cornwall,** 2 miles east of Bude, off A 39. This door, formerly that of the old gaol, is now in the south porch of the twelfth-century Church of St Andrew. It is 5 ft 6 in high and 2 ft 6 in wide, and studded with 240 hand-made square-headed nails, 120 of which in double lines form the word CLINK, colloquial for 'prison' and much used in the West Country to denote a small one-man or two-men lock-up.

(Bottom right) **Stillingfleet, Yorkshire,** 6 miles south of York, on B 1222. The finest specimen of ancient wrought-iron strap-work on a church door (that of St Helen) still **in situ.** (There are other notable examples housed in the Victoria & Albert Museum, taken from their settings in the interest of preservation.) This specimen is obviously the work of a blacksmith imbued with the Norse tradition: it shows a longship with 'steer-board' and other such features, and ornate hinges terminating in the traditional Viking dragon-head. There is another, but lesser, specimen of such a door in the south porch of the Church of All Saints at Staplehurst in Kent.

(Top left) **Scarrington, Nottinghamshire,** 8 miles east of Nottingham, on A 52. This 'Horseshoe Obelisk' is composed of some 35,000 discarded horseshoes, systematically laid in courses one above the other with their 'toes' turned outwards and the old nails left in. This has resulted in their knitting so firmly together that the village smith, a man named Flinders, who started the obelisk in 1946, has raised it to a height of over 14 ft on a base 5 ft in diameter at ground level; it tapers to about 3 ft at the top, where it is rounded off to a cone surmounted by a neat finial composed of three interlocking and balanced horseshoes. The whole edifice stands rock steady.

(Top right) **Falmouth, Cornwall.** This curious detached chimney stands alongside the Customs Quay, overlooking the motley shipping in the harbour. Known as 'The King's Pipe', it was built for the Customs men to burn contraband tobacco smuggled through the port. Brick-built, in four decreasing tiers on a stone plinth, it stands some 30 ft high. It is ugly, strictly functional—even though today it is no longer called upon to serve as an outsize pipe for the consumption of tobacco illegally brought into the King's (or Her Majesty's) domain.

(Bottom left) **Askrigg, Yorkshire.** Wensleydale, in which this most attractive village lies, has for centuries been the home of the delectable commodity known as Wensleydale cheese. Today the cheese is largely factory made, but formerly it was produced by the wives of the dale farmers. This is a specimen—rare nowadays—of the stone-and-wood cheese-press used in the process. It is to be found standing, a little forlornly, in the garden of a farm cottage half a mile outside the village. Its threaded bar is sadly rusted, its timbers eaten away, which is not surprising, for this cheese-press started work in the seventeenth century. Its stonework, however, is as good as new.

(Bottom right) **Eyam, Derbyshire,** 5 miles north of Bakewell, on A 6010. This is a mechanically operated sheep-roasting spit, which is to be found in an enclosure just short of Plague Cottage, where, in 1665, the Great Plague of London reached Eyam and the Rev Mompesson consoled his self-isolated flock until it abated. The spit is used annually at the end of August or in early September at a ceremony that draws visitors from all over the Midlands and much farther afield.

(Top left) **Blythburgh, Suffolk,** 3 miles west of Southwold, on A 12. Clock-Jacks, or Jacks-o'-th'-Clock, proliferate on the Continent, notably in Germany, but are comparatively rare in England. There is a charming fifteenth-century specimen in the Church of the Holy Trinity, a church out of all proportion to the modest size of the village it serves. In painted wood, rather less than life-size, this quaint figure originally struck the hours and announced the entrance of the priest. Today he stands silent, save when the curious visitor plucks at the cord that makes him strike the bell with his hatchet-like hammer and at the same time jerk his head to one side.

(Top right) **Wishford Magna, Wiltshire,** 5 miles north-west of Salisbury, off A 36. This unusual group of plaques, set in the south-east corner of the wall surrounding St Giles Church, records in 'gallons' the varying price of bread over the past century and a half. No one seems to know at whose instance they were installed. Wishford is the setting for the traditional Grovely Festival, on Oak Apple Day, so perhaps it has an in-built desire to keep records, however out-of-the-ordinary they may seem to us.

(Bottom left) **Wolverhampton, Staffordshire.** This so-called Bargain Stone stands in the south-east corner of St Peter's Collegiate Churchyard. About 5 ft high, irregularly shaped and slightly concave on the east side, it has a hole near the top that is just large enough for two hands to be clasped through it. The name derives from the tradition that, in less sophisticated times than these, vendor and purchaser, or others with a pact to agree on, sealed their bargain by clasping each other's hands through the stone.

(Bottom right) **Burton Joyce, Nottinghamshire,** 5 miles north-east of Nottingham, on A 612. This is the topmost section of the spire of St Helen's Church, struck by lightning in 1890 and never replaced. It now stands in the angle of the south porch, in a condition which suggests that it is safer at ground level than on high! This church, like that at Stillingfleet, Yorkshire, is dedicated to Helen, daughter of 'King' Cole, whose name is commemorated in the name Colchester, and in the nursery rhyme. There is a similar, but larger, 'grounded' spire alongside the largely dismantled Church of St Andrew in the City of Worcester.

Shell House, Dartmouth, Devon, 10 miles south of Torquay. You will locate it in Lake Street, on your right as you descend the hill into this small town, in a narrow road parallel with the main road. For eight years or so its owners have been covering exterior and interior walls alike with every shell they could lay their hands on. They started with local beaches, then went to Wales, and then farther afield in search of the exotic. One small room alone contains no fewer than 40,000 assorted shells, arranged in complex, often beautiful, patterns, some of them geometric and conventional, others portraying in miniature local scenes and beauty-spots, such as Butter Wharf, Ferry Slip and Bayard's Cove. Conchologist you may be; but though you may recognise mussels, winkles, cockles, dog-whelks, sting-whelks, scallops, razor-shells, cowries, oyster-shells, limpets, slipper-shells, ormers from the Channel Isles, tiger-cowries and pelicans'-feet—that is only a beginning! The owners now estimate their tally of shells in every room, staircase included, not in thousands but—in hundredweights! They are enthusiasts indeed; no mean artists, either.

Shell Rooms, A La Ronde, Exmouth, Devon, between Lympstone and Exmouth. Locally known as The Round House (though it is sixteen-sided), this is an oddly attractive Regency **Cottage orne,** built in 1798 by Jane and Mary Parminter in imitation of a Ravenna church. From its central octagonal hall radiate eight wedge-shaped rooms containing possessions of the Parminter sisters (whose descendants still live here). These include handiwork in embroidery and also designs in shells. The hall rises some 35 ft to the Shell Gallery, with its diamond-shaped windows and exterior balcony. Though the portraits, samplers, pictures in seaweed and feathers and other improbable materials, and the cut-paper silhouettes so delicately executed, may hold the attention, it is primarily the shell-work that remains in the memory. It is used both as setting and as subject in room after room: ornate, fantastic, maybe, but so rich in imagination, so lively in its scope, so deft in its execution, that it invites appreciation rather than dismissive comment. This subject acquires a more than passing quality when it is discussed with the descendants of the eighteenth-century Parminter sisters, who so clearly cherish the heritage handed down to them.

The Rufus Stone, Cadnam, Hampshire, 3 miles from Cadnam, 10 miles west of Southampton. This unusual memorial stone lies in a New Forest glade a quarter of a mile from the dual carriageway north of Cadnam. It is a triangular bronze column standing about head-height. Bearing the date 1841, it has stood for well over a century after replacing a badly mutilated stone that commemorated the death of William Rufus. On one of its three faces is the inscription: 'Here stood the oak tree on which an arrow shot by Sir Walter Tyrrell at a stag glanced and struck King William the Second, surnamed Rufus, on the breast, of which he instantly died, on the second day of August, Anno 1100.' On another face the inscription reads: 'King William the Second, surnamed Rufus, being slain as before related, was laid in a cart belonging to one Purkis and drawn from hence to Winchester, and buried there in the Cathedral Church of that City.' On the third face of the obelisk the inscription reads: 'That the spot where an event so memorable might not hereafter be forgotten, the enclosed stone was set up by Lord de la Ware, who had seen the tree growing in this place.'

The Great Globe, Tilly Whim, Swanage, Dorset. On a sloping cliff 136 ft above sea level, about 1 mile out of the town to the west, this 40 ton stone sphere, 10 ft in diameter, is balanced on a small plinth. All about it are stone slabs that were inscribed with relevant information at the end of the last century when there was much general ignorance about geography and astronomy. You are informed, for instance, that in comparison with this globe, the Sun would be 1,090 ft in diameter, the Moon 33 in. The factual information is interspersed with uplifting sentiments in prose and verse by Shakespeare, Pascal, Milton, Dryden, Wordsworth, Tennyson and the Psalmist of the Old Testament. There are also anonymous offerings, such as: 'Let Prudence Direct You, Temperance Chasten You, Fortitude Support You'; and 'Let Justice be the Guide to All Your Actions'. This is Victorianism in stone. An intelligent modern commentary is implicit in the presence of slabs of local stone installed nearby on which the visitor is invited to do his name-scratching rather than on the Great Globe itself. The invitation has been very widely accepted.

102

Housesteads Roman Fort, Northumberland, 5 miles north-east of Haltwhistle. This is the best preserved and most interesting of the major forts spaced out along the 70 mile length of Hadrian's Wall between Newcastle upon Tyne and Carlisle. There are others, only just less well worth visiting, at Chesters, Carrawburgh, Chesterholm and Birdoswald, to mention a few only. Housesteads has been most skilfully excavated and it is possible to study its layout in detail—the granaries, latrines, administrative block, Temple of Mithras, and so on—and a clear impression can be gleaned of the actual way of life of the Roman legionaries who garrisoned these forts in the early centuries of the Christian era. The Housesteads Museum (like others at Newcastle and elsewhere) houses an immense variety of Roman relics: not only statues and other major finds but personal possessions recovered during meticulous excavation. Sometimes, however, it is the 'un-sung' detail that remains longest in the memory: this massive water trough, for example, at the south-east corner of the fort. Note the 'scalloped' edge of its near side. Why is this? It was not done for ornamentation, but is the result of generations of legionaries sharpening their short two-edged swords, with water handy in the trough for the purpose!

Roman Coffin, Soberton, Hampshire, 6 miles north of Fareham. This massive trough, 8 ft long and nearly 3 ft wide, was hewn from a solid block of stone and weighs between 2 and 3 tons. Standing now by the church porch, it was unearthed by a plough in a field nearby 100 years ago. Archaeologists declare that it is a Roman coffin, dating from the first or second century AD, and for this reason it was brought to this site for safe-keeping. Local tradition has it that 'the skeleton of a tall, soldier-like man wearing a toga and sandals' was found inside. This is highly improbable. But there is an additional 'occupant' well worth looking carefully for. You will find, at the wider end of the coffin, embedded in the stone edge, the fossilised remains of a scallop shell, a tacit reminder that the stone from which this enormous coffin was hewn nearly 2,000 years ago came originally from the sea bed, whence it was thrown up scores of millions of years ago, when England was part of the Continent of Europe.

George Fox's Preaching Stone, Firbank, Westmorland, 3 miles west of Sedburgh. The Founder of the Society of Friends, known more generally as Quakers, has left his mark, notably in the North Country. Born a weaver's son in 1624 and duly apprenticed to a shoemaker, he threw up his trade while still in his teens and thereafter travelled widely in Britain, Europe and America, preaching The Word. He met with rough treatment and was frequently imprisoned; but he had the gift of tongues and could draw enormous congregations, even in the unlikeliest places. One of these is at the top of a long fellside track that leaves the A 684 at the Black Horse Inn near the Yorkshire/Westmorland border and climbs steeply beyond the hamlet of Firbank, to level out among the heights. Westwards there is a stupendous view across the fells and valleys of Westmorland. Close beside the road stands a horseshoe of rock and drystone walling that encloses a stretch of smooth turf shaded by a stunted tree or two. A finely inscribed metal plaque inset in the face of the rock records that on Sunday, 13 June 1652 (when Fox was twenty-eight years old), he preached to a gathering of no fewer than 1,000 men and women here. His preaching on this occasion resulted in the inspiration to found the Society of Friends, for countless men and women went forth into the land, and overseas, carrying his message. Nearby, two small neglected graves introduce a note of melancholy into an otherwise inspiring scene, where life, rather than death, is the keynote.

Prince Chula's Dog's Tomb, Bodmin, Cornwall. It is not only the British, it seems, who are sentimental about their pets, especially their dogs. In the public (and happily at the time of writing free) car park in Cornwall's County Town there is this granite plaque 'Presented by His Royal Highness Prince Chula of Siam in Memory of His Friend JOAN, a Wire-haired Terrier who Died in 1948 in Her 17th Year'. Appropriately, there is nearby a dogs' drinking-trough, conscientiously kept full of fresh drinking-water, for the pets of townsmen and women and visitors alike.

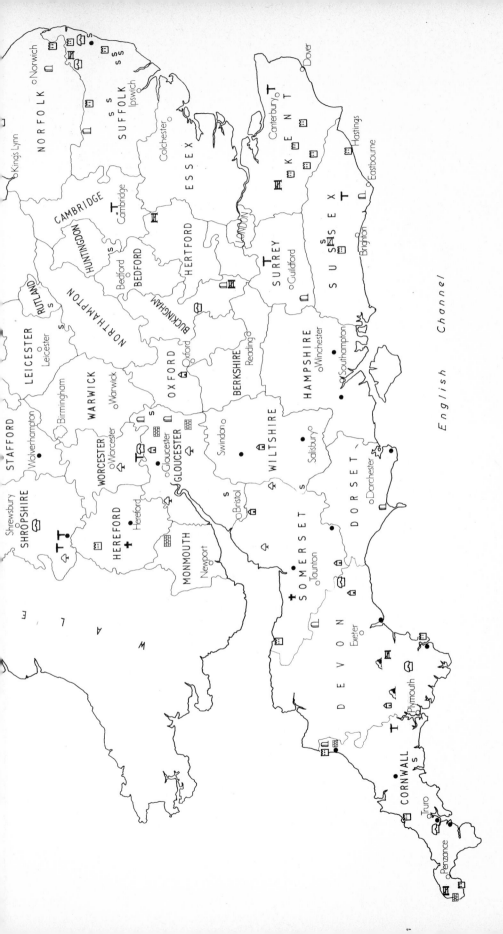

Index

Buckinghamshire
Lych-gate, Stoke Poges, 20
Thatch, Princes Risborough, 42
Tombstone, Stoke Poges, 48

Cambridgeshire
Milestone, Cambridge, 62

Cheshire
Inn Signs, Altrincham, Cheadle, Great
    Budworth, 26

Cornwall
Dog's Tomb, Bodmin, 106
Gaol Door, Stratton, 94
Hawker's Hut, Morwenstow, 82
House-in-the-Cliff, Porthcurno, 82
Huer's House, Newquay, 82.
Inn Sign, Lanreath, 28
King's Pipe, Falmouth, 96
Lych-Gate, St Just in Roseland, 20
Milestone, Callington, 62
Round Houses, Veryan, 76
Slate Wall, Stratton, 32
Stocks, St Feock, 92
Stone Wall, Sennen, 32
Thatch, St Feock, 42
Tombstone, Morwenstow, 50

Cumberland
Bowder Stone, Borrowdale, 66
Churchyard Cross, Gosforth, 52

Derbyshire
Lych-gate, Clifton, 16
Sheep-roasting spit, Eyam, 96
Stone wall, Thorpe Cloud, 34
Tombstone, Eyam, 46

Devonshire
Bowerman's Nose, Dartmoor, 68
Lych-gate, Ilsington, 20
Shell House, Dartmouth, 100
Shell Rooms, Exmouth, 100
Thatch, Totnes, 42
Toll Houses, Honiton, Tavistock, 10
Tombstone, Bampton, 48
Vixen Tor, Dartmoor, 64
Ye Olde Coffin House, Brixham, 82

Dorset
Great Globe, Swanage, 102
Tombstone, Broadwey, 50

Gloucestershire
Cider-mill, Cheltenham, 90
Inn Sign, Chipping Sodbury, 28
Inn Sign, Moreton-in-Marsh, 30
Stile, Guiting Power, 36
Toll House, Bishop's Cleeve, 10
Tombstone, Blockley, 48
Topiary Work, Micheldean, Sapperton,
    24

Hampshire
Roman Coffin, Soberton, 104
Rufus Stone, Cadnam, 102

Herefordshire
Belfry, Pembridge, 76
Churchyard Cross, Tyberton, 52
Cider-mill, Hereford, 90

Hertfordshire
Lych-gate, Anstey, 18

Huntingdonshire
Inn Sign, St Neots, 28

Kent
Gate House, Great Chart, 74
Lych-gate, Ightham, 16
Milestone, Sturry, 62
Oast-houses, Beltring, Goudhurst,
    Headcorn, Sissinghurst, 72

Lancashire
Stocks, Colne, 92

Leicestershire
Inn Sign, Market Harborough, 30

Lincolnshire
Churchyard Cross Shaft, Alkborough,
    54

Monmouthshire
Stile, Skenfrith, 36

110

Norfolk
Church Tower, Haddiscoe, 80
Church Tower, Little Snoring, 80
Tombstones, Ashby St Mary, 46

Northumberland
Roman Trough, Housesteads, 104
Toll House, Warden, 10
Tombstone, Warden, 50

Nottinghamshire
Grounded Spire, Burton Joyce, 98
Horseshoe Obelisk, Scarrington, 96

Oxfordshire
Toll Bridge, Eynsham, 12

Rutland
Inn Sign, Uppingham, 30

Shropshire
Milestone, Craven Arms, 58
Polissoirs, Stokesay Castle, 94
Signpost, Little Brampton, 56
Thatch, Leebotwood, 40
Topiary Work, The Lea, 22

Somerset
Churchyard Cross, Crowcombe, 54
Messiter's Cone, Barwick, 86
Polissoirs, Chedzoy, 94
Thatch, Yarcombe, 40
Toll Houses, Chard, Stanton Drew, 12
Topiary Work, Beckington, 22
Topiary Work, Cross, 24

Staffordshire
Bargain Stone, Wolverhampton, 98

Suffolk
Church Tower, Barsham, 80
Church Tower, Theberton, 80
Inn Sign, Farnham, 26
Inn Sign, Harleston, 30
Inn Sign, Southwold, 26

Inn Sign, Southwold, 30
Inn Sign, Snape, 26
Inn Sign, Snape Bridge, 28
Inn Sign, Stonham Parva, 30
Jack-o'-th'-Clock, Blythburgh, 98
Lych-gate, Barsham, 20
Round Tower, Wortham, 78
Thatch, Homersfield, Wangford, 38
Tombstone, Euston, 48

Surrey
Milestone, Esher, 60
Tombstone, Thursley, 50

Sussex
Cat House, Henfield, 74
Gannymede Model Village, Hastings, 84
Inn Sign, Bolney, 28
Lych-gate, Bolney, 18
Milestone, Horsebridge, 62
Tombstone, Jevington, 46

Westmorland
Preaching stone, Firbank, 106
Slate Wall, Ambleside, 34
Stile, Ambleside, 36

Wiltshire
Bread Plaques, Wishford Magna, 98
Inn Sign, Mere, 28
Maud Heath Memorial, Wick Hill, 88
Toll House, Devizes, 8

Worcestershire
Milestone, Bredon, 58
Thatch, Bredon, 42
Topiary Work, Kempsey, 24

Yorkshire
Cheese-press, Askrigg, 96
Church Door, Stillingfleet, 94
Dancing Bear, Brimham Rocks, 68
Stile, Askrigg, 36
Stone Wall, Slack, 34